The Win
2

Books by Shalonda McFarland

Non-Fiction

A Christian's Worst Witness...From Being Broke to Being Blessed

A Christian's Worst Witness Workbook

Marriage Maintenance Workbook

Praying with Purpose...A Foundational Guide to Effective Prayer

Fiction

The Win

The Win 2

Sunday Swap

Gag Books:

The Perfect Pastor

The Perfect Church

The Win
2

Shalonda McFarland

Purpose Praise Publishing, Houston, TX

The Win 2
by Shalonda McFarland

Purpose Praise Publishing
P.O. Box 62425
Houston, TX 77205 U.S.A.

Verses marked KJV are taken from the King James Version of the Bible, Public Domain. All other versions used by permission from Zondervan via Biblegateway.com

Cover Design by Vision Continued Custom Designs LLC,
Houston, TX
Author Photo by Paula Boykin, Jones Photo Creations

McFarland, Shalonda
The Win 2 / Shalonda McFarland

ISBN: 978-0-9885651-5-9

Library of Congress Control Number: 2020903721

1. Fiction 2. Christian Living 3. Lottery

Printed in the United States of America

C1

LAURA HAD BEEN lounging for over an hour in her oversized chaise, the pillows carefully orchestrated underneath her back just high enough for her to focus on her reading without being too low as to cause drowsiness to set in. The natural light from the window invaded the living room and illuminated the pages of her novel. She put the book down to fulfil the role of an audience of one for the blue jay who decided to make the limb on the oak tree in her and Frank's backyard its stage. Laura's smile and awe of the sweet melody that bellowed out of the small bird compelled her eyes to close so her ears could fully appreciate the bird's love song to its Creator.

Her mind began to recall memories. Memories began to flood her mind in such rapid succession, she didn't notice the songstress was long gone. A specific event lingered in her recall and came into focus as if she had slowly picked it up from a shelf just beyond a sheer curtain and brought it closer to view. Her face became pale and her eyes grew two sizes. Laura jumped up, dashed into her room to find her purse, and searched. Quickly unzipping the main compartment, she looked through each section of the medium-sized purse. Starting with the inner zip pocket she unloaded all its contents, went through them and finding nothing, put everything back. Systematically moving to the next section so she wouldn't forget what she had already searched and thereby having to redo it, she told herself aloud, "Pockets first. Left pocket, now right." Nothing. Using her hands like forklifts, Laura unloaded the bulk of her purse's contents. Annoyed at the receipts that, if she would have already recorded in her budget spreadsheet and thrown in the trash, wouldn't be getting in her way right now, she moved on to the checkbook; ruffling through every page. Then her wallet, every single section, and for no logical reason the zipper part that contained the coins, it wasn't there either.

Not knowing whether to be disappointed that she didn't find it or relieved that she mentally crossed off a possible spot from the list, she moved on to her nightstand. If she put it in there, there was only one place it would have been. Laura slowly opened the bottom drawer as if planning her attack. She dropped to her knees, then quickly to her bottom and inched up closer to the drawer, taking out one stack at a time. Stacks of magazines, notebooks, and papers she had the bad habit of writing notes on and then tearing off to save. She could hear her heart throbbing between her ears as she quickly yet meticulously combed for that one special piece of paper. Desperation completely filled her mind as she hoped and prayed the number she was thinking of was not written on it. This was all she wished for.

There was one last place to look. Laura opened the red notebook and pulled the flap open on the inner pocket. Nestled in the crevice was a small corner piece of crumpled-up paper with a series of handwritten numbers.

"Oh, thank you Lord, this is it," she told herself. "Now please don't match," she told the air. Examining the numbers as she tried to recall her exact movements so many months ago, she went into the closet and opened the safe to retrieve a copy of their winning lottery ticket. She compared the numbers on the torn slip of paper to the ones on the ticket, much like she had done that late night she'd discovered they had won. Back then she had compared the winning lottery ticket to a TV screen; now she compared that same winning ticket to a slip of paper that had been nearly forgotten, buried in the back of her mind and the bottom of her nightstand drawer.

Her eyes widened, "Oh Lord."

They were identical. Her body sunk into her chair as the weight of what this would mean to everyone in the lottery pool churned in her stomach and threatened to escape from her mouth. She of all people had broken one of the rules. How in the world would she tell Frank, let alone everyone else?

C2

TAMMY TOOK HER cell phone out of the pocket of her Betty Boop scrubs while at her desk looking over the notes on one of her patients. Her eyes moved from the chart to the silver-framed picture of her and Jerome on their wedding day, he holding her entire body in his arms, her arms around his neck. Her eyes quickly moved to the custom-made wedding ring that hugged her finger. She closed her eyes and leaned back in her chair, her head tilted to the side and a smile on her face. The buzz from her phone echoed from the desk laminate it laid on. Her smile widened as the word "husband" filled the screen. She scooped up the phone.

"Hey, I was about to call you."

"I made it. And Barbara says hello."

"That's not all I said," Barbara yelled in the background.

"Your sister's a mess. Tell her I said hello too. You guys have fun."

"Alright, I'll see you later."

"Bye."

Jerome placed his phone on his sister's round glass kitchen table as she came through the doorway with a bowl of sweet potatoes and a knife. She sat; her thin floral-print robe hung just below her knees. She started to peel. The two talked for several minutes and after a bit of catching up Barbara looked at him and shifted her body to take the pressure off of one side.

"So, did you ever find out what the prenup was all about?"

Jerome held a blank stare, so Barbara put the knife down and leaned back, her eyebrow raised.

"Uuhhh," Jerome started stammering. She had caught him completely off guard with the question, but he knew he should have been prepared. After all, he came to Barbara with his complaints and uncertainty during the engagement when Tammy insisted on getting a prenup, so the question was inevitable.

"No, don't do that. First, you hesitated, now you're stuttering, so you're about to lie to me. Don't lie to me Jerome. If it's none of my business just say, 'it's none of your business' and we'll leave it at that."

"Well, I'm not allowed to—"

Barbara's forehead crinkled.

"I mean," he rushed to correct himself, "I don't want to get into it. It was nothing…detrimental."

Barbara squinted her eyes, trying to read her brother's face.

"OK, it's none of your business," Jerome's grin accompanied a laugh.

"Fine, fine," Barbara threw her hands up in surrender and chuckled herself. She looked down to gather her thoughts and held her head back up, looking intently at her junior sibling.

"Jerome, you are married now. Your loyalty is now to your wife, not to me. I get it, and it's O.K. That's the way it's supposed to be. If you two have something going on that you don't want to tell anybody else, fine, honor that, and don't apologize for it. That's where a lot of marriages go wrong, when the person doesn't switch loyalties from their family to their spouse. She comes first now. Now that don't mean that you forget about me, but you have to attend to her needs first before anybody else's; that means even any kids that come along." She gave him a playful poke in the stomach.

Jerome shook his head in agreement, relieved that he was off the hook. "You give great advice for a single woman. You should get married again."

"I'll cut you with this knife," she joked. "No; been there done that."

"And got the t-shirt to prove it?"

"And I burned the t-shirt. I don't want any memories from that fiasco."

Jerome grunted and shook his head.

"I know marriage is not for me." She paused. "No, that's not true. The right man just hasn't found me yet and I am not about to lower my standards. I know who I am, what I want, and what I'm not gonna put up with." She pointed the knife at Jerome as if she were warning him.

"Whoa. Save that for the next man. I didn't do anything."

"Treat her right, Jerome."

"You know I will." He nodded emphatically, while wondering if he should tell his closest confidant that trouble was brewing in his new marriage. But how could he, when he wouldn't be able to give specifics. Before he got married, he used to tell Barbara everything;

they had no secrets. If it weren't so much against tradition, he would have had her as his best man instead of his high-school friend, Larry. He weighed his options, which were slim considering the consequences that had been spelled out to him. And he thought about what her reaction would be if he just flat came out and told Barbara that her new sister-in-law had won ten million dollars with four other families in a church lottery pool, and the effects of that were now eating away at the foundation of their marriage.

C3

LAURA PULLED UP to her parents' home and scanned the front yard, admiring the plush, meticulously manicured lawn her dad had undoubtedly cut recently. She picked her handbag off of the butter-cream leather seats and pushed the button to stop the engine. Walking the path to the front door she looked around the neighborhood and couldn't help reminiscing about her childhood; the spot on the curb where she scraped her knee riding her bike, the neighbor's window right across the street where her younger brother Maury and his friends hit a home-run ball right through the living room. And she could still imagine the white chalk that lined the squares of her and Nell's hopscotch game. She caught herself smiling, remembering how they had to constantly tell their brother and his friends to keep away. She realized that's what was missing on this street, noise, children laughing and playing. Those sounds had been swallowed up by years gone by and left with it an older generation settled in their routines. Even her parents' home reflected an earlier time and she wondered if they would use any of the money to make updates to the outside. As she studied the bricks and the archway of the porch, Laura was also grateful to have something unchanged in her life, a certain nostalgia that made her smile at its simplicity and pleasantness. She took out her key, rang the doorbell once, and opened the door. Her smile widened as the aroma of freshly-baked bread greeted her nostrils and temporarily closed her eye lids.

"Laura is that you?"

"Hi, Mamma."

"Hey, baby. You got here fast. The rolls are almost ready."

"Mamma, you didn't have to do that. I know how much work that is."

"That's what I wanted to do."

Laura shook her head in defeat. There was no use trying to chastise her mother for doing so much, she would do what she wanted to no matter what, so Laura just resolved to enjoy her mom's baking.

"Where's Daddy?"

"He's probably on his way back from the store."

Laura nodded.

"Sit down; I want to talk to you anyway. Your dad and I want to make some changes to our will."

"Oh, really?" *This doesn't sound good,* Laura thought as she pulled out the nearest chair and Maggy sat beside her.

"Are you going to be able to handle being the executor of our will?"

"Well yes, Mamma, we've already taken care of the most important things you and Daddy wanted done.

You both have told Nell and Maury how you want things split and who gets what so there won't be any surprises."

"Being the executor, it's important that you make sure all our requests are carried out, even if there are some you don't agree with."

"Right," Laura spoke with caution.

Maggy searched her daughter's eyes for any trace of reluctance before her next statement.

"We're willing the house to Maury."

"Wha—," Laura couldn't even get the word all the way out. She tilted her head, not quite sure if she heard her mom correctly.

"Laura, your dad and I have given this a lot of thought. We're up in age and tomorrow is not promised. If anything were to happen to either of us, your brother will move in—"

"For what, protection? A dog can do that." Laura's sarcasm was deliberate.

"Laura."

"It would be a constant frustration, Mamma. He barely comes to see you. Don't you see what he's doing? You just paid your house off. He's using this as an opportunity to live rent free, and you'll probably wear yourself out cooking all his meals too."

"Laura he's just had some bad breaks."

"Mamma, please stop making excuses for him. Didn't you learn when he tried to get you to cosign for that dumb Escalade?"

"Laura, this is different."

"If y'all would have been tougher on him growing up, he'd be more of a man now."

"Who are you talking to?"

"Mamma, I'm sorry for my tone, but mamma y'all been babying him since he was born. Just because he's the youngest doesn't mean he shouldn't be responsible. You should be harder on boys anyway."

"When you have some children, you can raise them anyway you want to."

Maggy leapt up to get the rolls out of the oven while Laura thought of another approach. She didn't need the money, selling the house would bring, she just hated to see all her parents' hard work go down the drain. Laura couldn't put anything past Maury. She knew Maury wouldn't take care of their childhood home and even though the house was paid for, he'd eventually find a way to lose it, either by not paying the property taxes or something else.

"Mamma, do you think it's fair to me and Nell to give the house to Maury when it was supposed to be split evenly between all of us?"

"Laura, I just want to make sure he'll be alright if something were to happen to us. You and Frank don't need it, and Nell and the kids are taken care of with whatever setup Paul has with the military."

"Why do we have to get penalized because Maury's not doing what he's supposed to do? He's going to junk it up, borrow against it, and lose the house, Mamma. We have a lot of memories in this house and you should will the house over to all three of us with equal share."

Ignoring Laura, Maggy continued. "I don't want Maury to know either, because I don't want him to get lazy or stop working."

"All of us need to know Mamma. Don't put that kind of stress and pressure on me. Nothing should be a surprise to anyone. And you and Daddy need to explain why you're giving something to someone versus someone else. And it's best if you ask each of us if there's anything we'd want inside the house; you know, anything sentimental to us that we could keep as a memory."

"Speaking of, I want to give you the doll set."

"That's very generous of you Mamma. I know how much those porcelain dolls mean to you, but Mamma I don't like dolls. They are nice and everything, but I do not want a collection of dolls. All I would do is sell it."

"That's fine if that's what you want to do with it. I want you to make sure that everything is appraised so at least you have the wisdom to know if you're getting a good deal on them or not. I want you to get your money's worth and do what you want to do with it."

Maggy handed Laura a warm roll she had just lathered with butter. Laura bit off a large chunk, not because she wanted to indulge in the light fluffy treat, but because it was best that she chew, rather than talk. She could swallow the roll much better than she could this news, and Laura was scared of what she might say to her mom next.

C4

ALL THE MEMBERS of the lotto pool sat around the massive table inside the offices of Brown, Roberts, and Dean Law Group for their quarterly appointment. After passing an embossed folder to each couple, attorney Roberts sat in the middle of the board room table and shared a silent glance with all the couples. Don and Janet sat to his immediate left, next was Craig and Amanda. Jorge and Maria sat opposite of him, then Jerome and Tammy, and Frank and Laura on his immediate right.

"I am proud of you. You are true to your word. Looking at what your accountant sent over, you haven't really touched any of the money. If you guys keep this up, the interest on your investments alone can sustain your families for generations to come. Jerome, since you're fairly new to this, I'll explain a few things. I work closely with their tax advisor and accountant to make sure we do things the right way. It's hard enough when one person wins the lottery but when you have a group of people, well that makes things even more complicated. And I've seen my fair share of lottery winners ruin their lives because of the decisions they made. I've also handled a handful of office pools from various industries. Now I've got to admit, this is my first time overseeing a win of a church lottery pool, but I've got to tell you, the way you've handled yourselves, I'd say you all have set the standard. Alright, we have a few things on the agenda today. One of which is you've decided now would be the best time to give the rest of the tithes and offerings to your church. Per your request, I've combined it all and it is reflected in one check. Frank and Laura, the portion you personally already gave is of course not included in this check. Also, per your request, the second check for your pastor will be included in a separate envelope but in the same package."

"I wish we could somehow be there when he opens it," Craig looked around the table.

"Oh, I'd love to see his face," Tammy agreed as the others threw in their sentiments.

"All those zeros…this is one package I'd like to hand-deliver myself. Your pastor is a blessed man to have you all in his church."

Heads lowered and half smiles slowly rose as they all considered the fact that they were just doing what they were supposed to do, and the true blessing came from the win in the first place.

"In your envelopes I've compiled a few back stories on some major lottery winners, one of which was right here in Houston. I'll tell you now, they all ended badly which you'll see for yourselves but my point in sharing them with you is to hopefully warn you, scare you if that's what it takes, so you won't make the same choices these people did. For the most part, these were pretty good people but once they got this money, they did a full 180. My suggestion is that you read them as couples and then discuss them all together."

"Jerome, as we discussed earlier, here is the confidentiality agreement I need you to sign. They did it all together so it's only fitting that you do the same, in front of everybody," Mr. Roberts chuckled.

Jerome recalled the steamy conversation with Tammy after their engagement, when she had first told him he had to sign the prenup. Then, after they were married, she informed him he'd also have to sign this agreement, to never tell anyone about the winnings. Because he felt like the group was running his household, he had lashed out, "I didn't sign the agreement, you did." And her reply wasn't much better with "Oh, so we're one only when it benefits you?" The day to actually sign came quicker than he wanted. Now he was the odd man out sitting in front of an already-organized group that was pressuring him into signing the contract. He hesitated. "Why are y'all so adamant about this?"

"Because one person can mess it up for all of us." Frank softened the blow by stating, "Not just you, but any one of us can threaten the entire group."

"I want to bless my sister."

"You can, you've just got to do it without telling her." Janet lowered the papers she was holding.

"But she won't tell anyone."

"That's what you think," Don readjusted his chair.

"That's what she'll be telling you after she tells your mother or her husband."

"What if she gets drunk one night and lets it slip out?" The comments shot from around the room.

"If people find out you'd wish you hadn't won it. It might not implicate us, but you'd be under all kinds of stress and be praying you don't have a heart attack or a stroke over the foolishness," Laura added.

"Everything they're saying is possible. One of my clients who won, well his brother and sister-in-law wanted him to put their three children in private school." Mr. Roberts shook his head. "People will ask you for things that they wouldn't sacrifice to do themselves."

You don't know anything about my sister. She's single and doesn't even drink. Fine, whatever. Jerome's thoughts seized his mind. He looked at Tammy who donned pleading eyes and a half grin that was both apologetic and full of hope. He grabbed the pen and made it official. "There you go."

"Very good," Their lawyer looked over Jerome's signature and walked back over to his seat and picked up another document.

"Jerome, now that you've signed, I can share with you Tammy's portion of the winnings." He walked back to Jerome with a legal-sized paper. "I'll explain a few numbers to you and the rest you can go over with your tax advisor. Lottery winnings are taxed like income, and since this win was such a large amount, it was taxed at the highest rate, 39.6%. The government takes 25% before you see any of it, and the remaining 14% is due at tax time. That's all been taken care of. And you'd better be glad you live in Texas, where there's no state income tax, that would be another 6%, roughly. What I want you to understand is even though each family's portion is $2 million, that's not your net; your take-home winnings. It's closer to $1.2 million. And after giving just your tithes, which actually comes off the top number, your gross, you're left with one million eight thousand dollars before you've spent any money on yourself. That's just an example. I'm not saying that's how much Tammy has,

I won't divulge how much money anyone has left, or how much money each family gave to the church as far as your tithes and offerings, that's your personal business. I just put it all together in one check and your pastor's love offering in another check. Any questions, Jerome?"

"No, I understand. I didn't realize the taxes were so high, but I get it. Almost half of what you win is gone right from the start."

"The point is, it only takes a few bad investments or large purchases and all your money is gone." Mr. Roberts held up three fingers and pointed to them one by one. "Buy a nice house, buy a vacation home, that's half a million easy, and one bad investment, and you're back to where you started."

Jerome looked at Tammy and nodded, reassuring her that she didn't have to worry about him; he wouldn't spend the money frivolously.

"Alright, the last thing is a reminder to look over your wills and let me know of any changes you want to make. Jerome, we do this at least once a year. You just let me know how you want to proceed."

Mr. Roberts looked around the table. "Unless anyone has any questions, we're done. Or course, call me anytime."

Each person stood, thanked their attorney, and approached Jerome with handshakes and hugs, officially offering their acceptance into their tight-knit group and into their lives.

C5

CRAIG HAD BEEN thinking long and hard about his offer to his son to pick any college of his choice after he did well at the community college but after researching the extreme fluctuation in costs of schools and in-state versus out-of-state tuition, Craig now had to change the parameters of his offer. Amanda never said anything but Craig had to keep in mind the fact that Joshua wasn't Amanda's biological son, and he had to make sure he was fair about planning for their other three children and the inflated costs they'd incur when they were old enough to go to college. Even more so, Craig realized he really wanted Joshua to live close so he could see him as much as possible, to make up for all the time they had lost, dealing with the shenanigans of Joshua's mother.

He made the call. Josh picked up on the third ring. "Hey, Dad."

"You sound winded what's going on?"

"Just a pick-up game with the fellas."

"Well, call me back when you can talk."

"I'm good. I was just leaving anyway."

"No, I need to have a serious conversation—"

"I'm all ears, really, I'm fine. What's up?"

"Josh, I know what I said at first about letting you go wherever you wanted to go to finish college but I've been looking at the costs of all these schools and the ones that are out of state and I didn't realize how much college costs. And we just can't do the out of state ones, but we can still do ones in Texas."

"But you said if I got good grades my first year, you'd let me pick any college I wanted to."

"I did, Josh I'm sorry, I misspoke. I didn't know—"

"I was just about to give you my top three schools."

"I know. I know. I was just too excited. We had just wo—" *won, are you crazy? What are you thinking?* Craig regrouped after almost letting it slip.

"Just what?" Josh's irritation grew.

"We had just...wanted...to bless you," Craig rolled his eyes at his own words. "There's something else. I wanted to see if you would come live with us while you're at school."

"So you changed your mind on the dorms too?"

"No, I'll still pay for the dorm, I meant between semesters. I'd like for you to stay with us during your breaks and in the summer."

"Uhmm, I don't know. Where would I sleep, your other kids have all the rooms filled."

"They're your brothers and sister, Josh. And we can make some adjustments."

"I don't know, mom may need—"

"Josh, your mom has had her time. I barely know you, but I want to. I want to spend time with you. And you need to see this side of your family."

"I've got to think about all this."

"OK. Let me know. And what were the three schools?"

"SMU—"

"Oh, no. No private schools. Did you even look at how much their tuition is?"

"Yes, but you said any college."

"You weren't trying to save me any money, I see."

Josh grunted, "Hey, you said you had it covered."

"There are plenty of schools, public schools, down here. I'd really like you to consider the University of Houston." Josh was silent. "And there's Texas A&M, UT even. Well, that's far away. TSU is right next to UofH, or Sam Houston is even close. Do some research on those schools and let me know."

"Yeah, OK."

"Hey, I'm paying for your school. Be excited."

"Alright, I'll talk to you later."

"Bye." Craig shook his head. The conversation confirmed Josh had picked up the entitlement attitude and ungratefulness of his mother. He hoped he'd be able to change the eighteen years of her programming and bring him back to reality.

C6

EVERYONE MET AT Frank and Laura's home as they normally did, not solely for business, but for camaraderie. They truly enjoyed each other's company. Don and Janet or Frank and Laura's homes were the destinations of choice since both were the most adult-friendly, neither couple having kids at home, which the ambience and décor confirmed. But since Frank and Laura's home was centrally located between all of them, it was the logical and most-chosen meeting spot. Their furnishings were so exquisite, they screamed to be used by adults. And they could be themselves, unfiltered in the comfort of their friends' home rather than any restaurant, even though they usually asked for a private room.

The living room looked like a picture from an upscale condominium brochure. Spacious, crisp colors of light-grey walls adorned a few paintings that resembled the work of Van Gogh and met maple hard-wood flooring bordered in crown moulding. Cream couches and chairs surrounded by platinum-accented end tables and a Versailles coffee table filled the space. The ambience of the room was inviting as well as breath-taking.

After dinner they convened in this room of choice to follow-up on the information their attorney had given them.

"Mr. Roberts had us read these sad stories in the hopes that it would keep us grounded so we won't repeat the same bad choices," Laura opened her folder.

"It certainly opened my eyes," Janet's eyebrows lifted.

"Before we talk about these lottery winners, I'm curious as to why you guys didn't do one big check from the beginning?" Jerome placed his hand on Tammy's leg.

"Because tithes and offerings are so personal, we didn't think to get together on that first," Amanda answered.

"Laura and I just so happened to give first but the ramifications of that made it problematic for everybody else to give after that."

"What do you mean?"

"We realized, if we all give separately, no matter how clever we try and do it, that would be four more big gifts which would lead to more speculation of multiple people being involved," Janet jumped in before Frank could answer.

"OK, I get it. How did this lottery pool start anyway?"

Don started laughing and tilted his head back as Laura crossed her arms.

"One day at church, my lottery ticket fell out of my purse and Don picked it up before I could," Laura said.

"Just being a gentleman."

"No, you were being messy. You knew what it was. You just wanted me to know you knew."

"What makes you think that?"

"Because of the way you smiled at me," Laura addressed the room, "you know that look people give you when they think they've caught you doing something or like they have something on you now, that's the smile he gave me."

"Oh, I'm hurt," Don playfully said. "The opportunity presented itself out of thin air, so I struck up a conversation with Frank about his wife's ticket, and there you have it."

"How did you know they would agree to a pool?" Jerome asked.

Don hesitated. "I didn't, but here we are."

"Yeah, so we invited Craig and Amanda and Jorge and Maria…I don't even remember how Tammy got in this thing, but we've been going strong for a while now."

"I don't remember either," Tammy's eyes narrowed. "We had to work some of the kinks out though," she added.

Jerome was intrigued.

"When we first started, I'd buy the tickets on Wednesday morning on the way to work or at lunch time so I could make a copy for Jorge and I'd hand them out that night."

"A copy, why not just text him the numbers?"

"Hey, I'm old school," Jorge held up his hands, "I want to see it on paper."

Maria added, "And at the time, he didn't get text messages."

"Who needs it? If I want you, I pick up the teléfono and call. I don't see how you young folks do it, so impersonal. My son, on Father's Day, he didn't call me; he sent me a text message, a text message! ¡Ay caramba!"

"OK Papi" Maria rubbed his back, trying to calm him down. "One time, Laura sent the message and took a picture of the ticket, but she sent it during bible study…"

"I had to work late that day and they're normally out by the time I sent the text," Laura defended herself.

Maria continued. "We had just dismissed but all of our phones went off at the same time so that looked suspicious.

"I had a brain freeze or something because I opened the message even though I knew it was just the numbers, and when I did, I thought the man sitting beside me saw it." Frank shook his head.

"We tried texting just the numbers but that was more of a headache because you start to wonder if Laura typed the right numbers in, so we went back to having the picture of the ticket sent," Tammy explained.

"Did you ever feel like you were disrespecting the church?" Jerome looked at Tammy for any signs in her face that his question was out of line.

"Not after all the money I spent trying to win that 60 inch flat screen they raffled off. They didn't have a problem calling out those ticket numbers in church," Craig sat back.

"OK," Amanda agreed while the others laughed.

Laura grabbed her set of papers their attorney had given them. "That's true. Alright, how about we just start with the first story and go in order?"

Heads nodded.

Tammy was the first to comment on the stories. "I don't understand how this man could just lose his mind like that and leave his wife for a woman half his age. I mean what was he thinking? He had to have known she only wanted him for the money, and he was dumb enough to leave his wife? I just don't get it."

"There are some men that would do that. And no, not all men are that stupid, if that's what you're getting at." Craig stated.

"He also made bad investment decisions. I mean why, when you have millions, do you take advice from someone who sought *you* out, to try and double your money? That's ludicrous." Janet shrugged her shoulders.

"He wasn't satisfied with what he already had. I agree that was a mistake." Don looked at his wife, knowing she would appreciate the double meaning of his statement, stemming from his past decisions that had once threatened their marriage.

"I know he had some major consequences, but nothing is worth taking your own life," Jorge held his chin and looked down at the floor.

"Let's move on to the next one," Amanda turned the page to the next story.

Laura shook her head. "The thing that gets me about this one is, he drastically changed. I can see how a garbage man would buy a mansion, I mean he did win $14 million, but then to start using drugs and buying very expensive jewelry…"

"Only to end up living off of unemployment checks when it was all said and done." Maria shook her head then added, "How terrible to waste all that money."

"Alright what about the lady who won $4 million but had to borrow money from a company that loans money to lottery winners and she never paid back all the money?" Don asked.

"See, what I don't understand is how? I mean you won the lottery and now you're borrowing money?" Jerome shook his head.

"She couldn't manage it." Tammy spoke up.

"Unfortunately, she's not the only one. That company wouldn't even exist if lottery winners didn't use their services. They specialize in it; lottery winners are their client base."

"And what about the man who bought cars for family and friends, bought a new house and turned into the party man only to end up taking a job paying minimum wage to support his six kids?" Amanda rushed on.

"Don't get me started on that one. He didn't even have the decency to put the money aside and take care of his family. That's lowdown," Jerome said.

"Just sorry," Amanda said with disgust.

"I got caught up by the woman who gave over two million of her money to charity, only to end up bankrupt," Frank recalled.

"She had a good heart but obviously didn't get the right financial advice," Laura said.

"Alright, this is getting depressing." Craig sat back in his seat.

"Exactly what I thought when we first read these. They blew a chance to do something great, to make major changes in their lives but they wasted it," Frank said.

"What a shame," Tammy said.

"So, what are the common themes here?" Don asked.

"Money didn't solve any of their problems that's for sure," Jorge interjected.

"No money management…"

"Greed."

"Changing your lifestyle." Answers shot across the room.

"Right, so we need to do the opposite. We need to really talk to our spouses and have a game plan about this. Of course, it's all personal. Me and Frank's aren't going to look like you and Don's."

Heads nodded.

"You know what all these people have in common?" Tammy looked around the room for the answer and after waiting a few seconds she gave it. "We know all their names…because they weren't anonymous."

Everyone's demeanor showed their agreement.

"You know there was a group of teachers who won and stayed anonymous." Amanda added.

"And we can do the same thing. We've done it so far. We just need to stay focused." Janet said.

"Don't buy a big purchase right behind another one," Don said.

"If you buy or give something to family, be very careful how much you spend." Janet said.

"Yeah, you don't want to do anything out of the norm that could raise any questions." Frank said.

"We can't help what happens at church because we don't have any control over that, but we tried our best to give the money with the least bit of interruption." Laura said.

"Right, we did our part, let God handle the rest," Amanda added.

"Yes, we did."

"He'll take care of the church."

Expressions and words of affirmation came from all.

After more small talk broke out around the room the group said their goodbye's and departed, each contemplating what they needed to do to keep their windfall and anonymity intact.

C7

FRANK AND LAURA headed to the mall to look around for some deals and see a movie in the early afternoon, before the prices went up and crowds increased. While in the car, Laura's phone rang, and she looked at the screen to see Maury's name. She rolled her eyes and put the phone back down.

"What, who is it?"

Laura smirked.

"Let me guess, your wonderful brother."

"He only calls when he wants something. I don't want to deal with that right now."

Frank shook his head and kept driving.

"You know Mamma and Daddy want to give him the house."

"What do you mean?"

"You know, when they die. They're changing their will to give it to him."

"That's not good. Why?"

"Same reasons for everything they do. They're worried about him making it."

"What are you gonna do?" Frank pulled into a parking spot.

"I don't know yet," Laura pursed her lips and they got out and started walking toward the entrance.

Once inside Frank motioned, "I'm going to go down here and look at some dress shoes. I'll meet you at Macy's when I'm done because I know you'll still be in there."

Laura chuckled. He knew her too well.

After searching the rows of shoes and deciding on two pairs, Laura combed through racks of dresses and pants. After over thirty minutes of trying on clothes, she got rid of the rejections by hanging them on the rack at the entrance of the fitting room and carried her selections over her arm and started searching for a cashier with a smaller line so she walked to the men's department. Frank rushed up to her and grabbed her.

"Laura, your dad's been rushed to the hospital."

Laura's eyes widened. She shoved the shoe boxes and clothes unto the nearest shelf and rushed to the exit with Frank.

"What happened?"

"They think he had a heart attack."

"What!"

"Nell called, but couldn't reach you. Maury called Nell after he couldn't get you. I called you like ten times."

"I forgot; I don't get reception in that store. I don't know why. What hospital?"

"Memorial Hermann."

"Downtown or The Woodlands?"

"The Woodlands."

Laura dialed her mom but got her voicemail. She dialed Nell, who picked up immediately. "Nell, what happened?"

"Daddy was cutting the grass this morning and he started having chest pains so bad that he fell to his knees. Mamma called an ambulance and Maury's up there now with her."

"We're on the way."

"I'm almost there. If I hear anything, I'll let you know."

"Alright, bye."

Laura looked at Frank, so he put his flashers on and picked up speed. She looked out the window and remained silent.

***

Tammy looked at the clock again. The ten o'clock newscast had just finished, and Jerome hadn't come home yet. He was increasingly staying at work late and it was frustrating her. They obviously didn't need the money so she couldn't understand what was going on. They were still considered newlyweds by most people's standards and after coming home from work she wanted to spend most of her time with her husband as she expected he wanted as well. Something wasn't right.

Tammy heard the key unlock the front door, so she straightened up from her slouched position on the couch. Jerome walked in and they exchanged greetings; Tammy waited for a kiss, but none came. Jerome went to the kitchen and poured himself something to drink, then headed to the bedroom.

She couldn't let this go on any longer. She would confront the issue. She followed Jerome into their room and thought about her approach to the subject.

"Jerome, you're working a lot of late nights. What's wrong?"

"If we finish the job ahead of schedule, we get a bonus."

"Do you really need a bonus?" She threw up her hands.

"No…and yes. On paper, with the win, no but I want to do this for myself. I like what I do and it's a challenge to see if we can complete this earlier."

"But we hardly see each other."

"It's only temporary. And the bonus goes to the whole crew. I mean every person will get his own personal bonus if we can pull this off. That's a big deal. I know they can use it. So, it's not just me we're talking about."

He paused, wondering if he should add to the conversation or not but decided to go ahead and bring up *his* issue. "Did you notice how when the lawyer talked to me, he kept referring to *their money*?"

She lowered her eyes. "Yes, I caught that. But what else is he supposed to say?"

"I don't know but it just seems…arrogant. I feel like I'm just a bystander or something, like I'm trying to enter your group's little world; like…" he searched for the right word "like an outsider, that's it. I feel like an outsider."

"Well, is there something I'm supposed to do?"

He looked away, gathering his thoughts. "I just feel…inadequate. I mean, you have all this money and what I'm bringing in is peanuts compared to that. I just can't compete with that."

"You don't have to. We're not in competition. Jerome, every man dreads getting a woman that's a gold digger, but you're upset because I don't need your money. I don't get it."

"See, that right there."

"What? I didn't say it with an attitude or anything, I just made a statement."

"It's like you hold it over my head. And you don't ask before you buy anything you just do it."

"It's not like I can't afford it."

"It doesn't matter you still need to consult with me. We should talk about it before you buy things."

"Why do I need to do that?"

"Because we're supposed to be in this together. I'm not talking about everything, but big purchases like anything over four hundred dollars."

Tammy balked. "That's nothing. I'll be asking your permission on just about everything."

Jerome shook his head. "You wouldn't think it was low if you hadn't won all that money. For an average household that is about right."

Tammy tilted her head. "But we're not an average household."

"But we're supposed to be spending like we are. And it's not about you getting my permission. It's about making decisions together." He searched her face to see if she was receiving what he was saying. "And you keep saying I. Don't get me wrong I don't want your money. It's just the spirit that you have about it all, just rubs me the wrong way."

"What spirit? And I don't hold it over your head. You know there are women out there who take advantage of their husbands, some don't even work. I used to hear them all the time bragging about how their husbands make sure they get whatever they want. Some of them are so selfish; they expect their husband to work two jobs, so they can have expensive things and you're complaining that you have a wife that doesn't need you to take care of her."

Jerome raised both hands. "That is the whole point. A husband is *supposed* to take care of his wife, but you're already taken care of."

"I didn't mean it like that," Tammy explained. "So…what, you want me to get my money and just give it away?"

Tammy's comment came so far out of left field and was so utterly ridiculous, he just looked at her, at a loss for words.

Tammy slowly leaned to one side and put her hand on her hip. In her mind, his silence gave the answer to her rhetorical question; he subconsciously resented the money and wished she'd never won it. Her eyes grew wider. "Are you serious? That's not an option." She shook her head in disbelief and stormed out of the room.

Jerome took a deep sigh and sat in a side chair. He wore a blank stare.

Tammy returned seconds later. "You didn't do anything to get this money I'm the one who had to work for this."

"You didn't work at all to get this. It was a draw. They drew the numbers and you just happened to win."

"No, I did a lot of work in order to put myself in the position to even be able to win. While I was working my butt off to get rid of those student loans, I made sure to pay every week in our lottery pool. I'm not giving this money up; this is *my* money."

"See that's what I'm talking about; you keep on throwing it up in my face. I know it's your money and

I don't want *your* money, but you don't have to keep saying it over and over again. You keep saying it like…like you have options if this doesn't work out. It's like you keep leaving the back door open just in case you need to walk out of it. But it won't be you walking out of it it'll be me if you don't stop this."

Tammy's mouth flew open. She couldn't believe what she was hearing. Sure, they've had an argument here and there but nothing of this magnitude. He had never said anything like this before. Her heart was bruised, his words jolted tears she didn't know could come so quickly. Instead of making things any worse she didn't say anything else but decided to leave him right there. She was done.

C8

"LISTEN TO THIS." Craig put his cellphone on speaker and pushed play on the voicemail while Amanda waited.

"I knew you weren't going to pick up the phone. Josh told me what you said. How are you going to offer something and then take it back? I think you're trying to control him. Just because you're paying for college don't mean you have the right to approve what degree he wants to take. And why are you making him work while he's in school. He should be concentrating all his time to studying." The next thing they heard was the click where she had hung up.

"He told her everything I said," Craig reflected back to each conversation he'd had with Joshua.

"You want me to call her back?" Amanda folded her arms and leaned back.

"Hell, no! Y'all both have bad attitudes and she's waiting for you to say something, anything. I'll take care of Gloria."

Craig walked into the bedroom and shut the door behind him so he wouldn't be sidetracked by Amanda's expressions, listening to his side of the conversation with his Ex. He sat for a minute and gathered his thoughts. He needed to prepare his mind so he wouldn't lose his temper. He also needed to brace himself for her next barrage of complaints.

Craig stared at the screen and scrolled through the list of missed calls until he got to the contact he named "Big Mistake" and clicked.

"You finally decided to call me back, huh? Did you listen to my message?" Gloria started right in on him.

"Yes."

"OK. Then, what's going on?"

"I already explained this to Josh. I'm not trying to control him. I'm trying to guide him. I'm not telling him what to major in, I just want to make sure he runs it by me, to make sure he chooses a profession that's going somewhere."

"And you're being too hard on him."

Gloria often changed the subject when she knew she was wrong or wasn't going to change his mind, so Craig had to follow her logic and guess what subject she was going to next. "By making him work through college?"

"Yes."

"How else will he have any work experience when it's time to graduate? How is he supposed to know what he likes and doesn't like if he's never experienced anything beyond fast food jobs? I'm teaching him to be a man. That's something you can't do. And if you would've worked with me instead of against me, he'd already be one."

"Don't start that with me."

"What else was he gonna do? You didn't set up anything. He didn't have any plans whatsoever. I pay for his college and all you do is complain about how I do it. If you want to pay for it, then you can do it your way, other than that, you should be grateful." Gloria was actually silent, so he finished with, "Is that it; because I've got stuff to do?"

"Fine, bye."

He uttered no reply. He was just glad the conversation was over.

***

Don heard the garage door open and quickly put down the papers that detailed his portfolio of investments. He had learned not to let it consume him, as it had in the past. He was now truly fulfilling Janet's request of spending more time with her. Her statement, *If you spent as much time studying me as you do your investments, you'd know me by now,* had really shook him up. And the time he had spent alone at the marriage counselor's office trying to figure things out had done wonders. After Janet agreed to stay in the marriage, Don thought the trouble was over, but he soon realized he still had much work to do. After years of dysfunction, now their marriage was healthy, and he couldn't be happier. He just regretted not being the man he is today before their children became adults and left home.

He greeted Janet at the garage-door entrance and took the grocery bags from her arms. After they both put up the groceries, they sat at the kitchen table.

Don grinned and reached for the Bible.

Janet shook her head, "What are you learning now?"

"The counselor told me to read Song of Solomon again."

"OK, you can recite something to me."

He reminded her, "But it's not my words."

She assured him by touching his hand.

"Your breasts are like pomegranates..." That line always made her blush. When he got to the word "fair" she made a face.

"Substitute another word," Janet said.

He briefly looked down and came back with, "Beautiful."

"Why don't you tell me that?"

"I don't know. It's like stating the obvious."

She tested him. "Even after all these years? What about my stretch marks and wrinkles?"

"You'll always be beautiful to me and I'll kiss every stretch mark that made my children possible. I'd rather call them love lines, and I appreciate every one of them."

She was speechless and looked at Don for a long time. "Where is my husband and what have you done with him!"

C9

LAURA JOGGED THROUGH the emergency room entrance of the hospital while Frank drove around to find a parking spot. After giving the name Tom Robinson to the woman at the information desk, Laura was directed to his room on the third floor.

The world stood still when she opened the door and saw her father laying there amidst an army of medical equipment. Her eyes were so fixated on this traumatic portrait, she was unable to move until she could hear the rhythmic beeps on the heart monitor, reassuring her that her father was indeed alive. Once that was confirmed, the sound of her own heartbeat descended in rhythm and softened its pounding between her ears. She was now able to decipher who was in the room and Nell stood to give her a comforting hug. Laura swallowed hard and walked over to hold her dad's hand. She leaned down and kissed him on the forehead, jerking her head back to keep the tears from escaping her face and falling on his.

"Hey baby," Tom whispered.

"Hi Daddy," was all she could say.

Laura glanced at her mother, who was silent.

Before anyone could fill Laura in, a doctor appeared. He acknowledged Laura with a quick head nod and started talking to Maggy and Nell. "We're still waiting on the results of the echocardiogram and blood tests and I want to do a heart catheterization too. As soon as we get the room prepped, the nurse will come back and get him. He's stable for now and we're monitoring everything. When he comes out of this test, he'll be in an actual room.

"Thank you, doctor," Maggy cupped her hands and started rocking back and forth.

"Laura, let's go outside so I can fill you in. And we're only supposed to have two people in this room at a time." Nell led the way down the hall to the waiting area where Laura saw Frank talking to Maury. She turned her attention to Nell.

"They already established he did have a heart attack. They did some tests that confirmed that. So now what they're trying to find out is how healthy daddy's heart is and how much blockage he has."

Laura shook her head. "But how, I mean, why did he have one in the first place?"

Frank and Maury walked over as Nell answered. "It could be anything; high blood pressure, cholesterol, stress." Laura folded her arms at the likelihood of the third reason and grabbed her bottom lip with her teeth and glanced at Maury, who slowly lowered his gaze. Frank monitored Laura's response in case he needed to separate her from Maury. She wasn't the type to be easily angered unless she felt like someone was taking advantage of her parents, and Maury often met that qualification. She had to stop her mind from racing to conclusions regarding any possible conversation Maury had with their father that may have triggered this. Right now, her sadness overrode any negative feelings she had toward her brother. She just wanted to focus her attention on their father and helping their mother in any way she could. She was just thankful her dad was alive.

C10

THE NEW SIGN at His Way Christian Church was twice as big as the old one, and digital. No more getting on a ladder to change the letters of the weekly saying one by one, now you just had to type in the saying and push submit. It could even display the current temperature of 97 degrees. Laura chuckled to herself because if it were up to her, she would put up a caption right after the temperature that said, *"If that's too hot for you, don't go to hell!"* She might just have to suggest that saying to one of the deacons. Frank was too busy contemplating where to park and decided to back into a space on the edge of the parking lot while Laura caught a wave from Amanda as she and Craig ushered in their children.

Once inside, Frank and Laura sat near the front as usual, just in time for the deacons to start devotion. The choir members were already seated, dressed in their deep purple robes this Sunday, the gold tassels matching the HWCC letters embroidered on the front. After the congregation echoed the praying deacon with a unified "amen," the musicians started playing the first choir selection.

Pastor David Wright and a few ministers appeared from the entrance on the side wall that bordered the choir stand and occupied the front seats on both sides of the aisle. Pastor wore a light grey suit that sported beige pinstripes. He topped his attire off with light brown shoes. He and the ministers were just as excited as the congregation to enter into corporate worship. During the fellowship period, Laura exchanged smiles and head nods with the other members of the lottery pool, but she didn't see Jorge or Maria.

The sermon was wonderful as usual and after the announcements, Pastor returned to the podium.

"Brothers and sisters, I need to talk to you today. It's been heavy on my heart and I've prayed about it and now I need to let you know about it. Is that alright?"

"Alright, Pastor," the lady in the big hat said.

"Talk preacher," a man in the third row shouted.

"Most of you remember when I stood up here and shared my joy over a donation we received and how we started a giving campaign. That was a tremendous blessing for our church. This whole community is enjoying our new youth center. It's beautiful." Claps and applause rang out. "I was hoping that donation would stir us up to be obedient and generous in our tithes and offerings. Well, I'm sad to say the tithes have actually decreased." Comments trickled throughout the congregation. "I'm actually saddened by that. Now listen to this…our membership has increased since I made the announcement. So, tell me how can our membership increase, but the amount of tithes decrease? You do the math. Notice I'm telling you this after we already took up the offering because, I did not want you to feel pressured, so I'm talking about it now." He looked around the sanctuary. "What I want all of us to do is take a look at ourselves. Ask yourself, 'why am I coming.' If you're a new member, ask yourself, 'why did I join this church?' If it's not to serve the Lord, then you've come for the wrong reason. And the best way to serve him is through obedience. That donation shouldn't have changed your obedience. We need to check our hearts this morning. This church, every church, is funded by our tithes and offerings. If you know anything about me at all, you know I don't do gimmicks. No fish dinners, no musicals. You can call this, the No Chicken Has To Die Ministry if you want to because we're not going to run the church like that. Don't get me wrong, all that is good if an auxiliary wants to raise money for a specific purpose, but the *church* is funded by your tithes and your offering. Now I want all of us to go home and search our hearts and decide this day if you're going to obey the Lord or not. Part-time obedience is disobedience, plain and simple. Amen?"

Amens resonated throughout the church.

"Come on now, I don't mean to be like Joshua, but you need to choose this day whom you're going to serve. You're either going to do it your way or His way. You do know what church you're in right?"

A trickle of laughter seeped in the congregation.

"For our name's sake…come on Brothers and Sisters. We've got to do better. The name on the marquee is a constant reminder of what our focus should be on. Now let's get it together."

Pastor Wright sat down while another minister came to the podium and offered the parting Benediction.

Everyone in the pool took it in. Many thoughts raced through their minds. *What will happen when the pastor receives the combined check for the church they just agreed to? Should they tell their lawyer to wait before he sends it?* Laura threw a concerned look at Frank then turned her head to make eye contact with Tammy. Tammy had the same concern written on her face and Laura turned back around before she called attention to either one of them. They would all definitely need to talk about that further.

C11

THE RING OF Frank's cellphone interrupted his morning newspaper reading. He looked at the screen and wrinkles appeared on his forehead. Something must be wrong for him to get a call this early. "Hey, everything alright?"

"Yes, hey. Well, not exactly. I need to talk to you," Jerome said.

"What's wrong?"

"I've got a lot of stuff that I'm dealing with. Questions, I guess. Just some things that aren't settling right with me."

Frank put the paper down to give his full attention.

"Why were you the one to break the silence? You know, on the trip. When was she going to tell me about the money?"

Frank stood and started pacing the floor. He couldn't dare let Jerome know that Tammy was originally not going to tell him about the win until they had been married for a few years. After all, she had changed her mind on her own, well with the help of the other pool members. But once she did change her mind, she was the one that eventually said she was going to tell Jerome on that trip. Frank just couldn't take the secrecy and tiptoeing around anymore, so he just nudged the conversation sooner.

"She was going to tell you on the trip. She even called Laura the night before to let her know. I just thought one of us might slip up and say something on accident, and ruin it. And I just couldn't take it anymore. We were drinking and having a good time…who knows what might have come out of any of our mouths at that point, so I probably panicked...there you have it."

Laura, hearing Frank's voice, awoke from her sleep and listened from the bed.

There was a long silence.

"I don't know, Man. This money, it…I don't know if it's good or bad," Jerome said.

"What do you mean? It's been nothing but good for me and Laura."

"Well, maybe that's because you both won, I mean together. But Tammy won this before I was even in the picture, and it seems like she's holding it over my head or something."

"How?"

"She just says stuff like, hinting around that it's her money and she doesn't need me."

"I don't know, have you talked to her about it?"

"Yeah, but she just doesn't get it. And I've been reading, you know the scripture where it talks about how His blessings add no sorrow. Well, if this money is causing friction in our home, is it from Him? I mean is it a blessing or not?"

"I hear where you're coming from, but that doesn't mean it's bad. Jerome, money isn't good or bad, it's just a tool, it's how you use it that counts. You have pro athletes and entertainers who have way more money than this. Some do right by it and some don't, but just because it's a lot doesn't necessarily mean you'll have sorrow. Plus, anytime you have a bunch of money *people* will give you sorrow."

"But I can't provide for her when she doesn't need me."

"That's just *your* hang-up. So she has money, get over it. Come on man, women make more money than men all the time. That doesn't take away the fact that you're still the provider. Shoot, Laura makes more money than *me*, way more, and I'm not bothered by it. It is what it is. I'm still the head of the house. And I'm still responsible no matter what. So regardless of how much money Tammy has it's still all on you. She may be a little guarded because y'all haven't been married that long and you know women are kind of leery—"

"But you don't know how it feels. I had to do the prenup, then the paper saying I can't tell anybody, and I had to do that one in front of all of y'all—"

"You're right, I don't know. You're probably feeling like less than a man or something because of all the rules but maybe what your problem is, is that you want to be in control. You think you're not in control, but don't look at it that way. Recognize the blessing that this is and think about all the decisions *you* would have had to make if it was you and not Tammy, who had won the money initially. That's a lot; don't put any unnecessary stress on her. She was stressed enough from not telling you. You and I both know how manipulative men can be, sneaking in and getting in good with a woman and doing everything right for a while to see what she has and what they can get from her. I know you've warned your sister about men like that because I have, well not a biological sister, but sisters at church. Man, just be happy and chill. So your ego's been bruised. OK, I get it. No, I don't understand exactly how you feel, but I get where you're coming from. Listen Jerome, I know you don't want Tammy's money, I can tell—"

"See, there you go, Tammy's money. Everybody keeps saying it and thinking it. But if we're married, isn't it supposed to be our money?"

Frank grunted. "I see your point. You're right. I'm sure one day y'all will get there. Don't think of it like that though. I mean she has to protect herself too, you know. Sometimes things don't work out, or husbands don't turn out to be what they say they are…I don't think that's the case with you, but you've got to put yourself in her shoes. Just be patient."

"Alright man, I appreciate it."

"OK, no problem. Later."

Laura approached with her hand on his back.

"Oh, was I loud?" Frank asked.

"No, I needed to get up anyway."

"That was Jerome."

"I figured. Frank, I need to tell you something." He had seen that look in her eye before and he dreaded whatever she was about to say next.

"The numbers that we won with…well they weren't computer generated…they were numbers that I picked."

"What? Wait a minute, what?"

"I know. I just realized it, well not too long ago. I just didn't know when or how to tell you."

"Wha—how? Are you sure?"

"I'm positive, Frank."

"But what about—"

"I know, the rules, right, I was supposed to say something if I chose the numbers instead of letting the computer do it. I was going to, but it was late that night, and when I texted everyone the numbers, I forgot to tell them that particular line of numbers I had chosen myself. And then after we won, I forgot to check. I wasn't thinking about that then."

"Why did you choose the numbers anyway? You always told me you hated doing it; that it was a waste of time because you never knew what to pick?"

"I didn't really."

Frank tilted his head, waiting for an explanation.

"Frank, it was the weirdest thing. I wasn't even thinking of the lottery and the night before I went to the corner store, the numbers just came in my mind, I was just daydreaming really, and I just wrote them down. I figured it couldn't hurt so I just played them."

"Well, I don't care. We won, so don't worry about it."

Laura's mind raced. "How am I going to tell them?"

"Who?"

"Everyone in the pool, Frank." Laura's agitation was obvious.

Frank shook his head emphatically. "No, no no. You can't tell anyone. You can never tell."

Laura's eyes questioned why. "Laura, you don't know what that would do, what they would think. They may not care that your numbers won, but they may think you feel entitled to a bigger chunk of the money or something. Trust me, leave well enough alone."

Laura wasn't so sure that was the best thing. She had messed up and she felt it only right to be completely honest with everyone. It wouldn't change the fact that they *all* had won, but at least they would know the whole truth.

C12

"YOU CAN SIT your things in here," Craig motioned to Josh.

As he opened the door for Josh to enter the room, Josh surveyed the landscape. It looked nothing like he expected, although he guessed he shouldn't have expected much. Craig had already told him he could use his younger brother Craig Jr.'s room anytime he came to live with them during his semester breaks so Josh knew the room wouldn't look like a dorm but the toys and gadgets, although nicely put away, made him feel like he was an intruder.

"Are you alright with this?"

"Yes, but I feel bad kicking Little Craig out of his room each time I come stay, that is if it works out and I decide to stay," his voice trailed off.

"It's OK, really. He likes having a big brother around and he'll be fine sleeping in the bunk bed with Caleb."

"Yeah, but having to share a room with your five year old brother is…a lot."

"They're only four years apart. And maybe now Caleb will actually sleep in his own bed instead of coming in our room in the middle of the night."

"OK, well thank you."

"Alright, well Amanda's almost finished so if you want to wash up and come to the table, the plates will be ready in a minute."

Dinner was nice but Joshua wasn't used to sitting at a six-person table, nor was he used to young kids doing what young kids do when they have company. He thought they would be playing around at the table, but they spent most of their time talking to him and asking him questions. Caleb, although the youngest, was the most talkative of the bunch. He had no filter, asking Josh things like, *why are you sleeping in my brother's room, and don't you have a house of your own?* Christina was very entertained and kept laughing at both her older and younger brother but kept her eye on Josh, as if she was trying to figure him out. Josh realized that he had missed a lot over the years and that maybe it would be nice to spend some time with his siblings so he wouldn't seem like such a stranger to them.

After dinner, Craig and Josh reviewed the three schools they were going to visit that week.

"Remind me which school is first."

"University of Houston, then Texas Southern, and Thursday is Sam Houston."

"Sam Houston is about an hour drive. Do you want to take a picture in front of the statue?"

"No," Josh shook his head, clearly amused. Taking a picture in front of the 67 foot figure of the general was the last thing he wanted to do.

Craig was overwhelmed that Josh seemed to finally be wising up and understanding what he had been trying to show him all along. When Josh received rejection letters from both Texas A&M and the University of Texas because of his low GPA, he realized that he didn't have as many options as he thought he would, and Craig's offer looked that much nicer.

"Daddy, I need to ask you something," Josh waited for Craig's approving head nod before he continued. "Why didn't you want me to live with you when I was younger?"

"I don't know what your momma's been telling you but, that's not true. I tried to get you to live with us. She wouldn't let you. Your mom tried to make my life pure hell."

"Why didn't you take her to court?"

"How many times?" Craig threw up his hands. "She took me to court at least ten times in these eighteen years, all behind trying to get more money, and I told the judge that she wasn't letting me see you like she was supposed to. I might as well have kept my mouth shut. All he did was remind her of her obligation to adhere to the court order, but they didn't enforce anything. And I didn't have any grounds to take you from your mother, from the court's perspective. The bottom line is the courts are not fair to the fathers. They only want to get you in the system and take your money, but they don't enforce the mother's duty to grant visitation. These 18 years felt like a jail sentence son; don't ever get yourself in that situation."

"But she said you were behind on paying child support and so you shouldn't be able to see me."

Craig shook his head. "That's not true. I was behind twice in all those years, and one of those was recently. Now I did purposely stop the first time because she wasn't letting me see you, but that didn't change anything. They just started taking it straight out of my check."

"She said you quit your job so you wouldn't have to pay."

"Josh, some men do try and skip from job to job to avoid paying but that's not me. I can see she's filled your head with a lot of lies. You don't have to believe me, just think about it for a minute. Does it make sense to quit my job when I have a family to provide for, just to keep from providing for you, my own son?" She's trying to make me out to be a dead-beat but it's not true. That's part of the reason why I don't want her nowhere near me.

***

Laura and her siblings listened to the doctor explain the procedure he was about to perform on Tom, a procedure deemed necessary due to the earlier test results.

"As I was explaining to your parents, there is risk with any surgery but I perform this surgery often so you have nothing to worry about, your father should be fine. Right now, you have too much blockage to risk not having this done," he directed at Tom, who shook his head in agreement. "It's called an angioplasty with a stent or what's also called bypass surgery. I'm opening up the artery so blood can flow through. I'll be using a catheter that has a balloon attached to the top. I'll insert it into the blocked artery and inflate the balloon, which opens the artery. And to help keep it open, I'll insert a tube. After surgery, you'll need rehabilitation which lasts several weeks. You'll need to come in for exercise sessions that we'll need to monitor. We'll also need to talk about medications, stress management, and your diet." He smiled and touched Maggy's hand to reassure her.

Laura looked at Nell and Maury. Nell mirrored her worried gaze, but Maury kept his eyes on their father. Laura noticed Maury's leg shaking. Even though this surgery was performed by doctors on a routine basis all over the world, they all knew the great risks involved. This could very well be the last time they'd see their father alive. When Maury realized Laura noticed his leg, he stood and walked over to Tom and touched his shoulder, then he headed for the door. Just as he reached for the knob he quickly turned around as if he had forgotten to take something with him but instead of going back to his spot, he went back and kissed his father on the forehead, then left the room in silence.

C13

BECAUSE OF WHAT Pastor David revealed at church, the pool wanted to get together to decide if they should hold off awhile before having their attorney send the checks. They all gathered at Frank and Laura's home. Before Laura got started she blurted out, "Guess what guys? Jorge and Maria won't be here tonight; when I called Maria I had to leave a voicemail. And she texted me back that they're in Mexico. They left last week."

"I noticed they weren't there Sunday," Janet crossed her legs.

"You noticed that too, huh? Amanda added.

"Why didn't they say something?"

"They're probably just super focused and want to hear from the lord, not us. Because we want them to stay of course," Amanda chimed in.

"Wait a minute Amanda, what exactly are you talking about?" Frank asked.

Amanda looked at everyone. "I thought you knew. They're not on vacation. They went down there to start the groundwork for their ministry." Don leaned back in his chair and the others had their own response.

"This shouldn't be a surprise. They told us months ago that they were thinking about it."

"Yeah, well that explains a lot. On the voicemail I told her what happened at church and on the text back she said whatever we decided to do, her and Jorge were fine with it."

"I just wish they would have said something, this is kind of a shock," Tammy said.

"Well, we all have to answer our own calling. If God told them to go, we've got to accept it and just pray for them and the people he sends their way," Craig responded.

Heads nodded.

"Right. OK, so what do y'all want to do about the check to the church?" Laura asked.

Don sat up. "I don't understand how all of a sudden the tithes go down."

Frank shook his head. "It's psychological, I guess. People think they don't have to do as much because someone else will pick up the slack."

"No, that's just flat out disobedience," Laura said. She had to catch herself. Because of the winning ticket numbers, that she alone had submitted, she felt like she was the pot calling the kettle black since she went against the very lottery pool rules she helped establish.

"I agree. It shouldn't matter what someone else gives or who gives a donation to the church. That doesn't stop you from doing what you're supposed to do," Tammy folded her arms.

"I don't know," Frank acquiesced.

Jerome kept silent. He didn't feel like he had a say in the conversation anyway, since it wasn't his money.

"OK, to your point, then we shouldn't need to reexamine what we already said we would do with the money. We can't worry about what's going to happen either. All we can do is do what's right. We gave our tithes and offering—"

"And Pastor's love offering," Janet interrupted her husband.

"Right, so we've done our part," Don concluded.

Craig shook his head. "All we can do is trust that God gives the pastor wisdom."

"OK, you're right. I'm fine with that," Laura looked around the room. "Well, from everyone's demeanor, we'll just leave everything the way it is."

Frank nodded and stood. "Good, come on fellas, I need to show you something." All the men left the room to go see, unbeknownst to them, Frank's new purchase, a seventy-five inch television he just added to his man cave.

That will hold them for a while, Laura thought. "So ladies, what's been going on with you all?"

Tammy whispered. "I really need to talk to y'all, I need some advice."

Everyone intuitively leaned closer.

"Jerome and I have been having problems. At first, he was happy that I won the money, but now he seems like he's resentful. It's like he's used to struggling and wants us to continue to struggle, like he doesn't understand how it feels not to struggle."

The ladies threw in their own experiences then Tammy said, "Maybe we got married too soon. I thought I knew him but maybe I don't."

Janet touched her knee. "Tammy, time does not matter because they change after they marry you. Sometimes they only show you what they want you to see and conceal who they really are until after you get married."

"Maybe you just overlooked the signs he was giving you when you were dating," Laura said.

"Well, what kind of signs could I have possibly looked for?" Tammy looked at them.

"Well, what is he doing exactly?" Janet's sessions with her and Don's marriage counselor came to mind.

"I don't know I just sense a resentfulness because I have all this money. I guess because I don't have to depend on him; but it's not because we won the lottery that I don't have to depend on his money. I worked hard before we won, to make sure I'm self-sufficient."

"It's probably because he feels you don't need him," Janet responded.

"I do need him, just not for money…and I think he wants me to give the money up."

Mouths dropped open but Laura responded with "What?"

"He actually told you that?" Amanda bent her neck forward.

"Why? That makes no sense," Janet added.

"No," Tammy addressed Amanda, "not the actual words but he didn't say anything when I suggested it. And not saying anything means yes that's what he really wants me to do."

Janet shook her head. "Just because he didn't say anything doesn't mean he actually wants that. He probably just didn't know what to say to your absurd suggestion."

"Why would you say that anyway?" Laura's hands were in the air, accenting the question.

"Giving up your money is not an option—"

"And no man in his right mind is going to give back free money," Amanda interrupted.

"Exactly. So many people pray to win the lottery and you did it, so you're not going to give the money up. You need to think about something else. What was his issue, the real problem?" Janet pressed.

"He feels threatened by the money."

Amanda's face wrinkled so Tammy explained more.

He says I keep holding it over his head, but I don't."

"Well, he said it for a reason, what else did he say?" Janet pried.

"I think he feels left out. He mentioned how awkward he felt signing the agreement with all of us in the room watching him. And he said I act like I don't need him....and I don't for money, anyway. But I don't flaunt it or anything."

It was a while before anyone spoke. Janet broke the silence. "You really need to be careful about this. Men need to be needed. That's just the way they are."

"And I can only imagine what he's going through. I can see from his body language, he's kind of reserved right now, but when we first met him he was really outgoing," Laura said.

"You're definitely in a special situation, and all I can say is try and put yourself in his shoes. And he's a man, you know they have big fragile egos." Amanda said.

"Don't let this put a wedge between you. Really think about what he's saying because most men don't complain much, so there's something he's really concerned about. Just really think about what he said and if you need to make some adjustments in how you act, or your attitude about it, the words you use, I don't know what it is, just pray about it. Most couples have fights about money because there's not enough, and you guys are fighting because you have too much." Janet rested her head in her hand.

"And that money's not gonna keep you warm at night," Amanda teased, in an attempt to lighten the mood.

"Well, it can," Tammy perked up. "It can pay for a good heater and it can also pay for me some good batteries."

"Oooh, Tammy, no you didn't," Amanda shot back after her loud laugh burst out from her belly.

Choking on her own laugh, Tammy added, "And now I can afford to buy in bulk. Yeah, I can get a subscription to a battery delivery company."

They all got a much needed laugh out of it and talked a bit longer until the men's voices grew louder, signaling their return.

Laura's heartbeat started pounding so loud she looked around at the ladies to see if they could hear it. She had decided since they were all here, what better time than now to reveal what she had done. After the men got settled, she stole a quick glance at Frank then turned her attention to their company.

"Everyone listen…I need to tell you something."

Frank caught Laura's stare and knew what she was about to do. "Laura, let me talk to you." He jumped up, pulled her by the elbow, and rushed out, heading into their bedroom.

Confusion shown on the faces of everyone. An awkward silence chilled the room. *What on Earth is going on,* Amanda's look questioned Tammy, who shrugged her shoulders in response.

"Laura, what are you doing?" Frank immediately lashed out after he closed their bedroom door.

"It's only right that they know the truth."

"No, they don't need to know. Laura, we talked about this already."

"I know that, but I disagree. And I feel so guilty."

"You're not thinking straight. What is this going to accomplish? It's just going to cause a rift between all of us. They'll be thinking about it, and who knows how any one of them is going to react or look at you differently. I don't know. You may be feeling guilty, but what do you think will happen after they know? Then every one of *them* will start feeling guilty. They'll think that this pool didn't really win anything, that you did it all by yourself."

"But that's not true. I wouldn't have even been at the store if it wasn't to fulfil my duties to the pool by buying all the tickets that day."

"Exactly, we're all in this together. You did most of the work buying the tickets each time and sending out the messages…you're entitled to mess up, nobody's perfect."

Laura considered what he was saying but didn't know if she could let it go. She didn't know how she could forgive herself for such a mistake. He was waiting on a response, so she appeased with, "OK, Frank."

"Fine then, leave it at that. Look, I know you've got a lot on your mind with your dad and everything, so you've just got to trust me on this."

Laura looked down.

"Laura, you don't have to agree, but I'm asking you as your husband, to trust me. Now promise me. Promise me, you won't say anything. No hinting, no nothing," Frank insisted.

"OK, Frank," she took a long deep breath and looked at him with eyes full of doubt. "I promise."

"Thank you." He reassured her with a hug. "Now when we go out there, we've got to tell them something. Actually, you need to. If I start talking, they'll know I stopped you from saying what you actually wanted to say." He looked around their bedroom for answers. "Just tell them about your dad. It's not like you're lying Laura, you're telling them the truth. Just tell them how he's doing and how the money has blessed them."

Laura shook her head in agreement and gathered her thoughts.

"You ready?" Frank had his hand on the doorknob.

Since winning the money, Laura had become very acquainted with acting, during church and with her family. And she was about to give another believable performance, but to the very people she never expected to. "Let's go."

C14

AMANDA RETURNED THE gas pump handle to its holster and pressed the receipt button, only to be answered with the digital words "cashier has receipt." Annoyed, she reached inside her car and grabbed her purse to go inside. Making note of the pump number and taking her keys out of her pocket to lock the doors, she turned toward the building only to stop temporarily because of a crowd of people coming out of the station all at once. They looked like a herd of sheep that had broken through a gate. Someone was holding a news camera and a tall thin woman wearing a nice blue contemporary suit, held a microphone. She waved her hair behind her shoulder and shook her head to the man holding the camera. It was then that Amanda noticed the letters KTRK and the ABC 13 Eyewitness News icon on the van parked on the side of the building, making the vehicle partially visible.

"They must have gotten robbed, now I've got to walk through a circus," Amanda said under her breath.

After standing in line to retrieve her receipt, Amanda took a deep breath to will her way through the distraction near the entrance. As she attempted to get through the door more people started walking in so she had to wait, but she could hear the woman reporter speaking. "The anonymity law has just started in Texas but the winner of the latest jackpot of ten million dollars figured out how to stay anonymous even before the law took effect. If you remember, they bought the winning ticket right here and the store owners have made some renovations to this station with some of the proceeds of their share of the fortune, and we hope the winner was a resident who has given back to this very community where their lucky numbers changed their lives. This is Robyn Rogue, reporting live, back to you, Bob."

Amanda's eyes bulged out of her head. She pretended to scrutinize her receipt as she walked back toward her car, her head lowered, scared to show her face, as if her expression alone would reveal to the world, she was one of the winners. She jumped into her car, put on her shades, and pulled down the sun visor; anything to make her feel hidden from the world.

***

Pastor David pulled up to Cynthia's Kitchen for him and his pastor friends' Saturday brunch. He could see by the vehicles in the parking lot that they had already arrived. He put his dry cleaning receipt in his pocket and tucked his mail under a towel laying on the passenger seat and started toward the door.

The smell of sweets tantalized his nostrils as soon as he opened the door; the aroma of cinnamon, nutmeg, and butter, saturated the air. Instinctively his mouth watered; proof the Pavlovian theory applied to people as well. He looked over the crowd and found his party at a table in the back corner of the famous cake shop, ordering their drinks.

"Morning brothers," Pastor David sat down.

"And what would *you* like to drink?" the waiter asked.

"A cup of coffee, with cream and sugar."

"I'll have these right out."

"How have you been Pastor Wright?" Pastor Anthony asked.

"I've been doing well Pastor Anthony, how about yourself?" David walked toward him and shook his hand.

"Mighty fine, mighty fine."

"Pastor Henry, Keith, you fellas been doing alright?" Pastor David shook their hands as well.

They both answered their affirmations and all four of them sat and looked over the menu.

"What you having today, Doc?" Pastor Keith asked Pastor David.

"Oh, let me see. Lemon bars…coffee cakes, hmmm, cookies 'n cream cupcakes, I haven't tried those. Ooh, key-lime-pie cupcake. I think I'll have one of each," he joked.

After the waiter returned with their coffees and lattes he took their dessert orders and the pastors commenced their conversation once more.

"Don't you have a revival in two weeks?"

Pastor Anthony shook his head. "Yes, I'm looking forward to it. It starts on a Wednesday and ends Friday. We have three preachers coming from out of town to bless us."

"Nice, we're having a musical that week," Pastor Henry reached for a napkin. "What about you Pastor David?"

"We're laying low for the next couple of months, just church and bible study. Pastor Keith what about you?"

Pastor Keith smiled. "Do you really want to know?"

Pastor David looked at everyone to make sure he hadn't missed something, then back at Keith. "Yes," as he chuckled the obvious response.

"Our church is taking a trip to Coushatta."

Pastor Anthony almost choked on his latte. He started coughing, trying to catch his breath.

"Are you OK?" Pastor Henry leaned over and hit his back.

"Lord have mercy, Jesus. You can't be serious," Pastor Anthony regained his voice.

"Yes, I'm so serious. I told y'all we'd be taking one when we met at Pastor David's that time. We're spending three days over there. And yes," he looked directly at Pastor Anthony, "we're staying at a resort that has a casino and we're gonna go gambling."

"Well, good for you. I hope your church has fun," Pastor Henry took a sip of his coffee.

"OK, let me know how that goes," Pastor David was intrigued.

Pastor Anthony shook his head. "Brother, I think you're making a terrible mistake. I just don't think it's right associating the church with a casino trip."

"I know exactly how you feel about the issue, you've made that clear…and I disagree. I don't see anything wrong with us going to have fun. There's no difference than spending our money on a bowling trip. That's what we want to do. The women's group came up with the idea and I think it will be fun."

"Neither one of you is going to persuade the other so let's move on," Pastor Henry suggested.

While Pastor Anthony closed his eyes and shook his head, Pastor Henry changed the subject, "Pastor, how's the new youth center doing?"

"Very well, thank you. I believe it's been a blessing not only to our church but to the entire community as well," David shook his head.

"Wonderful." Keith said.

"Pastor, I hear your congregation has increased in size, congratulations. You know how the word gets around." Henry was sincere.

"How much do you think the youth center had to do with it?" Keith asked. "I know the key to any ministry is having something for the youth, I'm just wondering if we're doing enough at our church to meet the need."

"And how do you think a gambling trip is going to help the youth?" Anthony wouldn't let it go.

Pastor Keith noted the sarcasm. "We can do both."

"Well, maybe you should focus more on the youth than taking the adults to go do something that may cause them to stumble."

"If anybody gets out of line, I'll make sure to send them to your revival when we get back."

Pastor David's eyes got bigger and he quickly picked up his cup and took a gulp.

Henry was less discreet, "Oooh."

Keith smiled at that.

Directing his energy to David, Pastor Anthony said, "A word of advice; make sure your congregation isn't growing because there is hype around the youth center and all the rapid church improvements. All of that's good, don't get me wrong, just make sure that's not the only reason why they are there."

"Awe, yes, in other words make sure they're coming for the word not the wallet; the church wallet, that is," Henry clarified.

"Now, I agree with that," Keith said.

"If that's what will get them there, I'm fine with it. By any means necessary. But you're right, the word needs to sustain them and I'm confident that the word will do its job, it won't return void. The youth center may get them there, but the word will keep them there." Pastor David said.

"Gentlemen, here's your order."

"Thank you. You're just in time. I don't think we could have gone much longer with these heavy discussions this morning," Keith joked.

Everyone started in on their desserts and changed the conversation to less weightier matters.

C15

PASTOR DAVID SAT at his desk in his church office, studying his upcoming sermon, as he did each Saturday after his brunch with his pastor friends, when his cell phone rang. He highlighted a sentence in his Strong's Concordance and placed it next to his Bible. He jotted a note on his pad and looked at the number displayed on his phone. After it rang for a fifth time, he sighed and pushed the accept button, then the speaker phone button.

"This is David." After no response, he tried, "hello?"

"Yes, Pastor David?"

"Speaking."

"Pastor, this is Sister Evella."

"Hi Sister Evella, what can I do for you?"

"Well, Pastor, I've got a real big favor to ask. I'm about to lose my house."

Pastor David sat back but said nothing. He already had an idea what would be coming next.

"The bank's gonna foreclose on my house if I don't come up with six thousand dollars by Friday."

"I'm sorry to hear that. What are you going to do?"

"I was hoping my church could loan me the money."

"I see." Pastor David put his hands on his face.

"Pastor, are you there?"

"Sister Evella, how did you get into this situation?

"I just got behind and couldn't get caught up."

"Who else have you asked for help?"

"I don't know anyone who has that kind of money."

"What about your kids?"

"I can't ask my kids for money, and one of them owes me a thousand anyway."

"I see at least one of them doesn't have a problem asking you for money."

"Well, I'm their mother, and I don't feel right asking my children."

I suggest you get that money back for one thing. It's your money, and now you need it. And if you explain it to the child why, they should give it back to you quickly. That leaves you with five thousand. And since they already borrowed from *you*, I'd ask to borrow a thousand on top of that. It never hurts to ask, they can only say yes or no.

"Hmmm," she thought.

"So at the least you're down to five thousand. I know that sounds overwhelming but if you look at it another way, you need five hundred dollars from ten different sources."

"What about the church, or you and Sister Wright?"

"Sister Evella, my wife and I, we won't be able to do that. And as far as the church, I don't make that decision on my own."

"What am I supposed to do?" Her voice cracked.

"Have you gone to social services or whatever you call those agencies?"

"No, I tried to get a loan from the bank, but they turned me down." Her cracked voice turned into crying.

"I'm sorry you're in this situation. You must be scared, and this may seem hopeless, but you've got to think. I know you are divorced, but do you have a boyfriend—"

"He can't help me, I already asked."

"At all?" *What kind of man is that*, he desperately wanted to ask. "Well Sister Evella, get to working on what I suggested, and I'll try to have an answer to you by tomorrow. Just stay after church.

"OK. Thank you, Pastor."

"I'm not making any promises. I'll get with the deacons and the leader responsible for that area and we'll see."

"OK. Bye, Pastor."

"But Sister, you really need to do everything you can. Leave no stone unturned."

"OK. I understand. Thanks again."

He clicked the end button and took a long sigh then stood and walked to the sanctuary and sat on the first pew, with his fingers interlocked and hands hung low, both elbows on his knees. The silence and darkness welcomed him.

Pastor David stayed in the sanctuary, thinking and praying for over forty-five minutes before he returned to his office. Before he could sit, his phone rang again.

"Lord, no more today, please." He looked at the screen and saw Pastor Henry's name and answered.

"Hey Henry, you alright?"

"Oh, yeah, I'm fine. I just wanted to call because I'm not sure I liked how the conversation went today."

"Which part?"

"David, you know my heart, and I'm not calling to talk about anybody, I just really want to know, how do you deal with Pastor Anthony? He's so negative and, I don't know just...well you understand what I'm trying to say?"

Pastor David chuckled. "Yes, I think I know where you're coming from. I've been asked before, why I continue to deal with him but what I've learned is sometimes you can learn more from someone who's opposite of you than you can with a like-minded person. It gives you different perspectives, you know. And he challenges me, that makes me be more grounded in what I stand for. And besides, who was it that said, 'you keep your friends close and your enemies closer?' Now, I'm not saying he's an enemy, but I'd rather hear the negative straight from him, than from what someone told me he said about me. I've got to give him credit, he may be set in his ways, but he's not a hypocrite. With him, you know exactly where he stands."

"I just don't know how to interact with him sometimes; he takes things so seriously."

"Well, pastoring is serious business. I know you know that, but he and I also feel more like mentors to you and Keith, so Anthony feels like what you two do are a reflection on him as well. And I feel that way too, to a certain degree. We both just want to see you two do well and avoid some of the mistakes we've seen young pastors make. We might not always agree on things and yes, he may be stuck in his ways, but he means well. Henry, I've been doing this for over twenty years. I've seen all kinds of personalities, just be yourself, and know what's best for you and your church."

"I see Keith doesn't have a problem standing his ground. I think some things he does on purpose."

"Probably. It's funny to me to see a young pastor like Keith stand up to him."

"That's true, OK, I just wanted to ask you that."

"Uh, Henry, before you go, let me ask *you* something. I want to get your take on this situation, maybe it will give me a fresh perspective. One of my members just called me asking for six thousand dollars so she won't get foreclosed on her house. What are your thoughts on that? And before you answer, yes, we've helped people in all kinds of situations in the past, but I want to know how you younger preachers handle requests like this."

"Pastor David, I actually learned this from an old preacher and it's really effective. One of the brothers asked the church for some money, I think it was three or four thousand. I don't remember if it was to save a house or a car but anyway, I had my secretary look up his giving record. You know he only gave fifty dollars for that whole year."

"Noooo."

"That's what I said. I thought the finance people had messed the books up or miss-keyed a number or something. I had them go back and look at previous years and in the five years he was there, you know that joker had only given seven hundred dollars."

"Each year, right?"

"Pastor, in all five years, that was all he gave total."

"Please tell me you're joking."

"I wish I was."

"So, what did you do?"

"I sat him down and had one of my deacons in there with me. I told him I was gonna give him all the tithes and offerings he'd ever given our church since he had been there. His eyes lit up and he was calculating in his head, thinking he was about to get a come-up, but when he looked at that check, he just sat there, face just as pale...He looked at me, and dropped his head."

"Did he take it?"

"Yeah, he took it. And that's the last time I saw him. He was too shame to come back. He knew what he was doing."

"Humph." Pastor David rubbed his chin and looked up at the wall. "I think you may be on to something. I need to make a phone call."

"Tell me how it goes."

"Sure will. Thank you." Pastor David ended the call and within seconds had phoned the church secretary.

C16

JEROME SAT HIS wife down on the couch. "Tammy, I didn't mean what I said."

"Out of the abundance of the heart the mouth speaks so yeah you meant what—"

"Tammy I'm trying to apologize. I know what the Bible says but sometimes we say things we don't really mean." He pulled her close. "I would never leave you, even if you cut off my foot, I still wouldn't leave you. I just *need* to take care of you."

"I've got that taken care of, so you can focus on something else."

Jerome pinched the top of his nose. "Tammy you're missing the point. There is no other job more important than taking care of you. That's my duty as a man. We've got to figure something out because this isn't working."

Tammy turned her head slightly, disturbed by his words.

"That's not what I meant. I told you that I will never leave you and I'm serious about that; we've just got to figure out something else with this situation."

"Jerome, there are plenty of women who make more money than their husbands and there are some stay-at-home dads. You can provide for me in more ways than just money."

"I'm not made that way; I could never stay at home while you go to work; that's out of the question. Even if you quit your job, I'm still going to work. And money is the primary way I provide for this household. Listen, I just need you to be more…"

"Respectful?"

"No, I just need you to tone it down. I don't need you to bring up the money every time we talk about a large purchase. And, well I guess respect is another thing because we still *need* to talk about the money. It's yours, and I'm fine with whatever you decide to do with it but at least give me the respect of discussing it with me. I want to be part of the decision process, not an afterthought once you and your buddies have talked it over without me."

Tammy sat there thinking, as she searched his eyes.

"Can you do that?" he asked.

Tammy couldn't remember ever making a decision with the pool then going to him after the fact, not while they were married anyway. They only time she could think of was when she decided to break the news to him about the win. Maybe he was talking about the last meeting at the lawyer's office. She forgot to remind him that he'd need to sign papers, but she didn't keep him in the dark about it, she had at least told him he'd eventually have to sign it, just like everyone else. Maybe in his eyes, that was enough. "OK, yes, I'll try. And I apologize if I made you feel like you weren't included. I want you to be part of everything I do…and have. But I need you to stop being so uptight about it. We won ten million dollars for crying out loud. Be happy about it. Don't be bothered by the fact that it happened before you came along."

"For the ride?"

"Whatever," Tammy rolled her eyes, "just enjoy the ride."

He pulled her closer into his arms and hoped that Tammy would really try to change, while she hoped he would get over his insecurities and just go with the flow.

***

Laura pressed play on her DVR and proceeded to watch the recorded news. She fast-forwarded through the commercials and pressed play again. She paced back and forth in the kitchen, moving from the refrigerator to the counters, getting her ingredients out to make spaghetti. While she started chopping the garlic into fine pieces, she could hear the latest calamities facing her city; another car-jacking, complaints of unfixed pot holes, theft, and a preview of who the World Series winning Houston Astros had lined up for their next few games. Then she heard something about the lottery, which got her attention. She looked at the screen to see the picture of the corner store and she gasped. The same place where she bought the ticket was being featured on the news. She wiped her hands on the towel and reached for the remote control. "Uh, Amanda!" Laura saw her walk out of the store, in the corner of her screen. Rewinding the footage to capture what she missed, she pressed play again. She listened intently to the lady holding the microphone.

"And what are the odds that the holder of this winning ticket helped this very community? There are so many needs with schools and churches right in this area.

Let's hope that they were generous with their windfall. They chose to remain anonymous so even though we may never know if they used the money for good, we are excited to know that the winning ticket came from our hometown."

A flood of guilt broke through the dam that Laura had built in her mind. The beep of the alarm system jolted her out of her trance. Frank came around the corner. Before he could get in the kitchen good, Laura spoke first.

"Our gas station was in the news again." Frank waited for more details, urging Laura with his eyes. "They're talking about the new anonymous law Texas just approved so they brought up the latest win, our win, that's why this Robyn lady is doing a story, and look, Amanda was there." She grabbed the remote again.

"Amanda didn't say anything did she?"

"No, she just walked out the store. She's only on the screen for a couple of seconds. You can tell she's trying to stay off camera."

Frank watched the whole segment. "OK, I don't see anything to be alarmed about." He could tell his words gave Laura no comfort. "Laura, we've been through this. So you bought the ticket close to the church, you can't change that. It's gonna be fine." He grabbed the remote and turned the TV off. He knew if he hadn't, she'd watch it over and over again, analyzing every second. He had a more pressing issue on his mind, one that had been bothering him for years.

Laura frowned but went back to cooking, seasoning the spaghetti meat that was in the pan.

"I'm going to confront my mom." Frank said with a sigh of relief. He was finally going to ask his mom why she had never told him who his father was, so he would have at least had the chance to get to know him before he had passed away.

"That's good. I'm so happy about that, that you're at least gonna talk to her." Laura lowered her voice and grimaced, "Before you go too hard on her, are you sure your father didn't know? I mean, him *never* knowing he had a son is a little strange. Nell told me Paul was the one who knew she was pregnant before she did, because he threw up one day at work."

"I guess I'll never know. She took that possibility away from me. And she didn't have the right to decide who should be part of my life, especially my own flesh and blood. I missed out on a lot, not having a father."

"She might have thought he would reject her or you, or thought she was trying to trap him."

"How is that trapping *him*? She's the one that got trapped. She had to raise me with no help. He was sleeping with her; he knew the chance he was taking of her becoming pregnant. Why do women try to make decisions for us men? The news media and these movies have you women thinking the worst. We want to do the right thing."

She threw her hands up. "I don't know, Frank. I'm just giving her the benefit of the doubt."

"One of my cousins called me and told me she didn't look too good, so I'm gonna go see her and while I'm there, I'm gonna get to the bottom of all of it."

Laura stopped what she was doing and went over to Frank, kissing him on the forehead. She was proud that after years of not talking to his mom, Frank was finally taking a step to see her. Even if it would be an unpleasant visit, at least he would see his mom and maybe get the answers he'd always longed for.

C17

AS SOON AS Sunday morning church service ended Ms. Evella made her way to the waiting area in front of the pastor's office. She sat alone and started picking at her fingers, biting away hangnails, waiting for the time to pass. The pastor's door was closed but she could hear the muffled sounds of him and at least two other people having a discussion. She leaned back in the chair, pressing her head against the wall, trying to get a clearer sound, but to no avail.

Inside pastor's office, the voices were quite clear, but it was mostly Pastor who was doing all the talking, or ranting, as Sis. Sheila, the leader over Benevolence, would say.

"Now she's been coming here over ten years and the records show she's given $10,650. Now I know what she does for a living and for her job people make anywhere between $30,000 and $50,000. Now you mean to tell me that in ten years that's all you've given to God?"

They knew not to give an answer to Pastor's rhetorical question.

"Now if she was just tithing alone, I'm not even talking about giving an offering or anything else, but if she was doing the bare minimum of what the Lord says, she would be giving $3,000 a year, and that's on the low end. So after ten years she should have given at least $30,000 and that's if she never got a raise. Instead, she gave about $1,000 a year; which would mean she only made a $10,000 salary for ten straight years. Now, come on, what do people think I am?"

Sis. Sheila dodged that question by looking at Deacon Johnson, but he only offered silence.

"You know what I want to tell her. My flesh wants to tell her 'no, you are not a tither.' Is she really a member?"

"Yes, Pastor, she is," Deacon Johnson said.

"She emphasized on the phone '*my church,*' like she's one of the biggest supporters. But she isn't supporting like it's '*her church.*' No, think about it. That's a question we all need to ask ourselves. I should ask the congregation next Sunday. 'Are you really a member?' Just because you say you're a member of the church doesn't make you one. If you join any secular organization, and say you're a member, there are certain qualifications you need to meet for your membership; you'll have to pay membership dues and abide by the rules, whatever they are, to keep your membership active and in good standing. Only in the church do we do whatever we want and still want the benefits of membership. People come late or don't come at all, don't contribute…they want God's help but won't do what His word says. And then when God is true to his word and curses them to where they're about to lose everything, they come running to the church, the very place that they neglected, and ask for help. Stop leeching off the church!"

"Pastor," Sis. Sheila whispered, "she's right outside, she can probably hear you."

Pastor shook his head and went over to his desk.

"Pastor, there are government programs that help people with food, utilities, and even mortgages. She may not have reached out to any of them, but I can give her the information."

"That's fine, but I still need to talk to her first. Now that I've got that out of my system, I can calm down. Deacon Johnson, will you sit outside, I don't want her to feel too outnumbered. Sheila, I need you to stay here, I don't meet with women alone, if I don't know them well. And Deacon Johnson, remind me to put something in place. I know my number is on the church website and I've also given it out over the pulpit, but I need to establish some sort of barrier. You deacons need to be the ones to filter these requests, it's taking too much time away from what I'm supposed to do. Ever since I announced about the donation, people act like we're a bank. It was supposed to encourage the people, not give them an excuse."

"OK, Pastor, I'll get with the brothers and we'll put a process in place. Are you ready for her?"

"Yes."

Moments later Sis. Evella walked in with a steady pace. "Thank you for seeing me, Pastor."

"Yes, Ma'am, please have a seat." He motioned to the empty chair Deacon Johnson had just vacated and he came from behind his desk, eliminating the symbol of authority, and sat beside her, in an attempt to make her feel comfortable. "You know Sis. Sheila, right? She's over the Benevolence and Helps Ministry so I asked her to join us."

Sis. Evella nodded her head toward Sis. Sheila.

"Sis Evella, first, I want to thank you for…" *he didn't want to lie and thank her for being a member because she wasn't adhering to the teachings,* "being consistent in coming to church," he mustered. "Again, I'm so sorry about your situation and I hope everything works out."

Sis. Evella noted his word choice and slightly shifted her head.

"I know you have a lot to do, so I'll get to the point."

Her eyes blinked.

"I've just got to be transparent with you. A lot of people come to the church asking for money, members and people off the street. They want to pay this or that because they got behind, and I've heard many reasons for why they get behind. So what is the church supposed to do? You know a lot of people say they have a money problem but what they really have is an obedience problem. See, the bible teaches us how to handle God's money and it tells us we'll be blessed when we do it His way, or cursed if we don't."

"And what does that have to do with me?"

"I pulled your giving record here at the church, Ms. Evella, and I truly believe the main reason you're facing this issue right now is you have been mismanaging your money and more importantly been disobedient in paying your tithes."

"How do you know? I don't always put my name on the envelope. And sometimes I pay in cash." She regrouped to focus on lowering her voice. "But that's not the point. I came to my church to see if I can get help. I come here every Sunday and I should be able to get some help when I need it."

"Yes, we're going to try and get you some help, that's why Sis. Sheila is here."

"Yes, ma'am, I have a list here, of a number of programs the city of Houston has in place for people who need assistance."

"I've tried those programs before, they want too much of your information."

Sis. Sheila inhaled. "Yes, they have limited resources and since they're giving assistance, you need to be willing to give them information so they can track the—"

Sis. Evella stood. "You know, I would think that my church would be able to give a longstanding member like myself some help."

"Sis. Evella, I'm sorry to disappoint you. I've got to be a good steward over everything that comes into this church. I will be praying for you that you'll be able to keep your house."

"Well, thank you. You have a good day." She placed the information in her purse and walked back out.

Deacon Johnson soon came back in and shut the door. "I guess she didn't take it too well."

Pastor was silent.

"I don't like her attitude. Pastor, there's something about her that's not setting right with me." Sheila picked up her purse and put her paperwork back into the folder "She felt entitled to that money even when you explained…" Sheila shook her head. "I don't know, I don't think we've heard the last of this."

C18

ROBYN ROGUE'S CAMERA man peeked his head around her office door, noticing the unpacked boxes on the floor of her newly painted office. Her door name plate hadn't even been placed yet. He waited until she put the phone down before interrupting but she saw him anyway. "Change of plans, Brent. Come listen to this." She held the phone up and wrote something on a notepad. He put the phone to his ear and Robyn pressed a button."

Brent looked down to concentrate on the voicemail message he was listening to, his eyes darted up at Robyn. "We may have a story."

Robyn, yanked the phone and put it in the holder. "I know we do." She glanced at her watch. "I'm not waiting until Sunday, most churches have Bible Study today, let's go see what we can find out."

"But the lady didn't leave her name."

"I don't need it. I've heard her voice. If she talks around me, I'll know it's her. A disgruntled church member may just have given us the biggest lead we've had."

"How do you know she was upset?"

"I can hear it in her voice. She's upset about something."

"OK, she mentioned a donation to the church close to the time of the lottery win, but it may just be a coincidence."

"Brent, there are no such things as coincidences in this business. And haven't you heard the saying, 'hell hath no fury like a woman scorned?' A donation out of the blue, a new youth center, and I just happened to have just done a follow-up story on anonymous winners." She smirked and grabbed her keys. "Let's go."

***

Robyn pulled up to the parking lot of His Way Church, but saw only a few cars there, it being a little after six in the evening. She parked on the outer edge of the parking lot.

Her forehead wrinkled as she looked around. "Brent, wait here." Before he could object, Robyn was out the door, leaving him with the sound of the blaring air conditioner.

Thirty minutes passed before Robyn emerged, briskly walking back to the vehicle.

"What happened?"

"The pastor wouldn't even come out and see me. When I asked to speak with him, one of the men asked me why and I told him. I waited while he went to the back. When he returned, he told me he was sorry, but the pastor doesn't want to do any interviews."

"So why are you upset?"

"He didn't have the decency to tell me himself. I'm a news reporter, he should be happy I even want to do a story on this church."

Robyn drove out of the parking lot and parked on the side of the street. "Let's go." She was out of the van before he could ask why.

"What?"

"Get your camera ready."

"For what?"

"His Mouthpiece told me the pastor would rather me not do any story on the church—"

"So what are you doing then?"

"He didn't say, 'don't do it,' he just said, 'he'd rather me not.' There's a difference."

"Why here, then?" Brent waved to the street and open field.

"Because I can shoot anything I want on public property. Now, I want you to zoom in on the church when I give you the signal, and make sure you get a clear picture of the sign."

"Robyn, if he doesn't want us here, then maybe we should go."

"If he doesn't want us here, maybe he has something to hide. And the public has the right to know."

Brent shook his head and took a deep sigh, as he retrieved his camera gear and got in position.

"After my broadcast, I'm sure he'll want to talk."

C19

PASTOR DAVID TOUCHED the button to retrieve his voicemail.

"Pastor David, this is Keith, I saw a newscast on the church man. You been holding out on us?" He laughed deeply. "Do me a favor; tell Ms. Robyn Rogue about our church's gambling trip. That's free publicity, man. And make sure you give her my phone number, I'll let her do a story inside the church. I'll talk to you later."

The corner of his mouth crinkled. Pastor David deleted the message and let the phone slide out of his hands, unto the side table of his living room recliner.

"What's wrong, Dear?" Loretta noticed his demeanor.

"Nothing I want to concern you with."

He didn't want to think about the news situation anymore but struggled to get the incidents out of his head, so he started a conversation he had been meaning to have for a while.

"Loretta, I know what I'm about to say may sound crazy and might not seem like the right time but I really feel led to quit my job and focus solely on pastoring."

She smiled. "It's about time. You really need to. I can handle the few bills we have. The house is almost paid off and I plan on retiring in a few years."

Pastor David got out of his chair to sit beside her on the couch. He wanted to ease the next part of his statement on his wife and felt she would take it better with him right beside her. "Honey," he grabbed her hand to brace her for his request. "Before you even ask, I don't know the answer and I can't tell you why…I want you to consider retiring early."

"I plan on doing it in four, maybe five years. That's not a long time. It'll be here before you know it."

He nodded in agreement. "I know, but I feel like you should make this your last year."

Loretta's hand recoiled. "What? How? Where is this coming from?"

"Like I told you at first, I can't explain it."

"What about the decrease in giving, aren't you concerned about that?"

"Yes, I am. I really am. But I have faith that it will all work out. We may have to hold on to the house note a bit longer, but I really need you by my side. You can be so much more effective if you're not burdened down with the pressures of your job."

"And you've prayed about this?"

"Yes."

She searched his eyes. "Well, you're gonna have to pray that He shows me too because I just don't see it. The numbers don't add up. I just can't—"

"OK. I will, but you make sure to pray too. Just be open." He kissed her on the lips and got up to get ready for the next day.

***

Frank pulled up to his mother's house. It had been almost three years since he'd seen her, even though they lived in the same city. He parked on the side of the narrow street even though the gate that enclosed the entire property, including the driveway, was open. He sat in his car for a moment and gathered his thoughts, his mind racing through memories as he surveyed the white wooden home nestled on cinder blocks. He opened the door and made his approach through the gate that stretched to the end of the driveway, walked under the carport, and knocked on the side door. Even though he still had a key to his mother's home, he knew it wasn't appropriate to use it. He waited.

The door opened without a question asked of identity even though there was no peephole or window at this entrance. He had a second of doubt that she was the one behind the door.

His bulging eyes were a substitute for the gasp he held in his throat, one that would seem rude if he were to let it escape his mouth. His mother was about eighty pounds lighter than the last time he saw her. Her once plump size sixteen figure had dwindled to a size eight at the most, even that he wasn't too sure of because a grey shawl covered her upper body and the house dress she had on was all but falling off of her.

"Hey son."

"Hi Mamma." Frank slowly ascended the three steps to meet her already-stretched-out arms.

"It's so good to see you."

"You too, Mamma." He hugged her delicately, enveloping her body with his arms, the touch confirmed what his eyes already realized, her stature was a fraction of what it was the last time he saw her.

"I was surprised to get your call. Is everything alright?"

Frank shook his head because, that was the question he needed to ask her. "No, I'm fine. Everything is fine."

"And Laura?"

"Yes, she's fine too." Frank looked his mom over. "What's been going on with you?"

"Oh, nothing much, just living one day at a time. It's so good to see you."

"Mamma, what's going on with you? You don't look too good. I mean you look…sick."

"None of us is going to live forever." She got up from her chair. "Wait here." She disappeared around the corner and reappeared seconds later with a long tin box. She unlocked it with a key and opened the lid. "If anything happens to me, I want you to know where all my documents are. I have an insurance policy." She lifted up the envelope. "My funeral and burial stuff is all here, I even have my head stone already paid for."

"You act like you're gonna die tomorrow."

"Tomorrow's not promised to no man. And, here is my bank account information." She put everything back in the box and locked it. "I keep this under my bed. When God calls me home, everything you need to know is in this box."

Frank wasn't quite prepared for this conversation, but he needed to press his mom on what was going on with her. "Mamma, what's really going on? Do you need something? Tell me, please. I don't want to hear it from someone else."

"Oh, it's hard to explain. It's in God's hands anyway." She talked slowly, as if every word was a chore to release. "Listen son, there's something I've been meaning to talk to you about. I should have done it many years ago. First, I need to apologize because I didn't tell you the whole truth. I really was trying to protect you though, but well…"

Frank broke his gaze and looked at the floor, not sure what would follow. Would she finally tell him why he was denied having a father in his life because she never told his father about him? *Whatever you tell me is still not going to change the fact that I grew up without a father, a man I never got the chance to meet.*

"Frank, your father did know about you. Please forgive me." Frank sighed. Finally hearing some resemblance of truth after a lifetime of lies, had knocked the wind out of him. He searched her eyes for a reason, although none she could come up with would ever justify the reason for him. "I thought not telling you who he was, was the best thing to do. When I was pregnant with you, I told him. At first, he told me you weren't his. When I assured him you were, he told me he didn't want to be a father and reached in his wallet and gave me three hundred dollars and told me to 'get rid of it.'" Tears slowly found their way down her face. She didn't wipe them away, instead she let them linger, accumulating at the bottom of her jaw bone while they slipped away at their leisure. "I told him I couldn't do that, so he said, 'don't ever ask me for anything then. I'm not paying for nothing because I'm giving you the money now to take care of it.' I, I couldn't breathe. I thought he loved me. I didn't try to get pregnant, it just happened. Anyway, he never answered any of my phone calls after that. When you were six months old, I took you to his apartment hoping that if he just saw you he'd fall in love with you. I didn't want to get back with him or anything; I was emotionally done. I just wanted you to have a relationship with him. He took one look at you and said 'Get that bastard out of my sight. I don't want to see him or you again.' Frank, I can't tell you what that did to me. I just couldn't…I cried for days, weeks, not for me but for you. I didn't understand how someone could be so evil, and to his own blood. So, I raised you on my own. He never gave me a dime. I didn't have the heart to tell you that your father didn't want to be a father. It would have broken your heart and I couldn't let you go through that rejection. I could barely stand it myself while I was pregnant with you. I didn't know what long-term affect it would have on you either, being rejected by your own father, so instead of putting you through that I never told you who he was. I know you didn't understand it then, and probably hated me for it, but I can take that. I'd rather you be mad at me, than to feel the hurt and pain by that man. I can't even describe to you what *I* went through and I would not allow that on my son. I didn't want you feeling like you weren't worthy of your father's love. I didn't want you to grow up feeling unwanted or less than. I just couldn't do it. Again, please forgive me, I did what I felt was the best thing to do."

Frank's tear-studded face matched his mother's, but regret punched him in the gut, causing him to burst out in uncontrollable bawling. All his emotions betrayed him, he could no longer hold any in. All the questions, all the time he'd spent daydreaming about doing things with his father, all the resentment he'd bottled up inside. His mind raced back and forth finding no rest. He realized all the bitterness and even hate he'd felt all these years were mistakenly placed on this woman who sat in front of him instead of the sperm donor who was his father. She'd sacrificed so much, not only to give him life, but to raise him into an adult. His tears were not adequate payment for all she had endured, especially what he himself had put her through. After some time, he got up and kissed his mom's forehead and cheek and held on to her diminishing frame. He refused to let go.

C20

AMANDA PUT HER keys on the counter and noticed an envelope addressed to her. She glanced at the return address and tore the envelope open. It was a letter from Jorge and Maria.

Hello Amanda. I know this is old fashioned, but I felt I should write you rather than leave a voicemail. I know everyone was shocked when we left and so fast. I will try to explain why we left and why we chose Mexico. First, why do you think we were blessed with this money? Yes, we can do what other people do, we can buy cars and vacation homes but then we would be like anybody else and we believe God and trust we have the opportunity to change the world not just change our lives with pleasure but really make a difference in people's lives, even those we don't know. Money goes a long way here, much more than in America, so we can help many more people. We're hearing all the stuff on the news all the bad stuff going on and we look at how much we have. We used to say what we would do if we had money, well now we do. We plan on opening a boys and girls club our church will operate. There's so many needs these kids have. We can't just not do anything about it. We challenge you to be different, too.

Here is a picture of the church being built. We were able to give jobs on that too. The community is very grateful we are here.

Make sure you share this with everyone else.We love and miss you,

Maria y Jorge

***

Laura pulled up to her parent's home, noticing the nicely manicured lawn, which was a bit higher than her father usually kept it. The thick lush grass looked like it belonged in front of a five-star hotel. She decided she may have to get the number of the lawn care service who did this job, for her and Frank's home. She was relieved that her father had agreed to give up that chore, not just for the time being, he had no choice in that matter, but for good.

She walked into her parents' home surprised to see her father doing exercises with a man in scrubs. The man was counting down, so she waited until he reached zero before she said anything.

"Hi, Daddy." She reached down to kiss him.

"Perfect timing, I need a rest. This man's trying to kill me."

Laura smiled and introduced herself. The man did likewise.

"I'm Mr. Robinson's in-house physical therapist."

"In-house? Daddy, I thought you were supposed to do your sessions at the hospital?"

"He did," her mom shouted from the kitchen, "but he didn't want to go back and forth three days a week, so we arranged for Mr. Steve to come here."

That's got to be expensive and probably not covered by insurance either, Laura thought but managed a smile. "That's nice, Daddy." She rubbed his shoulder and walked toward Maggy's voice. Maggy was at the kitchen table with her bible open, pouring over her Sunday school book with a highlighter. Laura hugged her from behind and kissed her cheek. If seeing her dad's personal help didn't shock her seconds ago, she was even more stunned to see Maury step through the door. He had come from out of the garage, through the door that separates it from the kitchen, and his shirt was drenched with sweat.

"You done, baby?"

"Yes, Ma'am. Hey, Laura."

"Good morning."

"I put everything back up, Mamma."

"We sure appreciate this."

"It's OK, really."

Laura looked at both of them, wondering what was going on. "What are y'all talking about?"

"Maury's been taking care of the yard for your daddy."

"Wow. I'm impressed." Laura looked Maury over, thankful he was actually contributing, but skeptical of his motive.

"It's nothing…really," Maury nodded off her complement.

"Mamma, isn't this home physical therapy pricey?"

Maggy leaned closer and whispered. "Yes, but we're using some of the money from our secret giver. Insurance doesn't pay for home visits."

That money was for y'all to enjoy. Why would you spend so much on private therapy when you can just drive him to the hospital? Laura could only muster a "hmmm."

As if reading her thoughts Maggy said, "This was important to your daddy. What's money for if you don't use it the way you want to; to better yourself, and make your life more enjoyable?"

Not the choice she would have made, but Laura had to respect it. After all, she couldn't get upset every time her parents bought something she wouldn't have. She needed to release the gift, or she was going to drive herself mad. Laura was silent. She slowly stood and walked to the edge of the living room and watched her father with the physical therapist. Tom was leaning against the couch trying to catch his breath, in his own home. He always tried to maintain his privacy so being able to fulfill his therapy obligation in his own house rather than a hospital or outpatient center must have been a relief to him.

"You know what Mamma, you're right." Laura squeezed her mom tight but felt the pressure leave her own body. She would no longer carry the burden of being watchman over what her parents did with the money. *What good is a gift anyway, if you don't fully release it,* she thought. It wasn't her job to monitor nor approve of how they decided to spend it. She had done her part. She had blessed them and that was enough.

Laura continued to watch her father work so hard to do each exercise the physical therapist prescribed. She was so fixated, Maggy shook Laura's hand, pulling her out of her trance. "Laura, can't you hear Maury calling you?"

"Huh? Oh, sorry." Laura turned to see Maury beckoning her from across the room. *Oh Lord, what does he want?* She walked toward him. *Lord, give me strength. I don't feel like dealing with his foolishness.*

After they got to the den, Maury closed the door behind them. "Laura, sit down, please."

Oh, here we go. Laura bit her lip.

Maury could sense her body language. "No, I'm not…" He gathered his thoughts and started over. "OK I know I've done some things in the past that I'm not too proud of…but this thing with Daddy really scared me Laura. And I don't want him to die because of me." Maury's eyes became glossy and he cleared his throat. Laura fought back the instinct to reach over and touch his knee, consoling him was still hard after all he had put their parents through over the years, but Laura had never seen her brother like this. She felt a bit uncomfortable but hoped his heart was sincere enough to impact his actions, consistently. Mowing the yard was a start, but way overdue. He needed to show some changes in other ways as well, especially his constant requests for financial help, when he being a single man, and the only boy in the family, should be the first to *offer* help to their aging parents, not the one who constantly drained them with his various schemes. Laura would have to watch and wait.

C21

ROBYN WOKE UP earlier than she normally would for a Sunday morning and sent a text to Brent, making sure he was getting ready as well. She stood in front of her closet analyzing which outfit she should wear. Her decision wouldn't be based on particular colors or style, but on practicality. She was on a mission. She decided on a navy-blue suit versus a dress. Although the dress would suggest a more innocent and approachable persona, she needed to be able to hide her small voice recorder and be able to discreetly reach to turn it on and off without attracting unwanted attention, which is what her suit jacket afforded her, having an inside pocket over the chest.

She reached for her red-bottom heels, the only thing in her wardrobe she was sure to wear today. She always felt powerful, unstoppable even, when she wore them. She needed that confidence to be bold enough to stand in the very church she had been dismissed from earlier that week, His Way Church. This time she wouldn't even ask for the pastor, she would mingle in with the congregants and talk to them. She would ask them questions; someone was bound to know something.

Her phone rang. It was Brent, letting her know he had arrived to pick her up. Robyn was adamant about him coming in his personal vehicle rather than the station van so their presence wouldn't be as noticeable. When they arrived at His Way Church, there were many vehicles in the parking lot. She had already filled Brent in on the plan so as soon as he parked the car Robyn hopped out, leaving him to keep watch and be ready if needed. She lingered in the parking lot, approaching one person after the next as they walked toward the building. Some of them responded with blank stares others with smirks when asked whether they knew anything about a lottery winner donating money to the church. She changed her approach slightly with each person and watched their reactions carefully. Some recognized her from the local news, others avoided her at all cost, and others dismissed her questions with a head nod or flip of the wrist. A few even voiced their disapproval of her being there, which she kindly ignored.

Joshua emerged in view after returning to the family van to retrieve his little sister's Bible. Craig and Amanda, and the kids were already inside. Robyn pounced.

"Excuse me young man. Do you know anything about a donation from a lottery winner?"

"Huh?" The question caught him off guard.

Robyn altered it, "Does anyone that goes here, win the lottery?"

"No, well, I don't know," he shrugged his shoulders. "I'm just visiting. What makes—"

"Thank you," Robyn quickly moved on to someone else. She didn't have time to explain, she needed to get to someone who knew something. This was a numbers game, the chance of finding the right person who would really talk and share useful information increases the more people you actually talk to, so she had to speak to as many people as she could.

Joshua stood there and watched as the reporter jumped from one person to the next, one family after another. He noticed some eyeing the woman as they approached the entrance and tried to avoid her altogether. He wanted to find out more, but Robyn avoided eye contact, so he went back inside and joined his family.

"Thank you," Amanda took the bible and gave it to little Christina.

"No problem. Who's that woman outside? She's kind of rude?" Josh looked at his father.

"What do you mean, what woman?"

"I don't know. She was asking questions about a lottery winner."

Craig and Amanda looked at each other. Both of them grew stiff but kept their composure, even though they desperately wanted to bolt out the door to see what was going on. They couldn't comprehend someone actually asking questions on a Sunday morning, right before church was about to start. "I don't know, it's probably nothing," Craig said.

"I'll be back, let me check them into children's church." Amanda rushed off while Craig and Joshua went into the sanctuary to be seated.

As soon as Amanda got the kids checked in, she shot a text to Laura then waited a few seconds. After no response, she punched her name in to call.

"Hey, oooh you just reminded me to put my phone on silent," Laura responded.

"Where are you?"

"Pulling up in the parking lot right now."

"Did you read the text?"

"No, I didn't even know you sent one. You need something?"

Amanda looked in all directions. There were too many people around. Everyone was in earshot so she couldn't take the risk of explaining more. "I can't talk; read it now before you get out of the car. Gotta go."

Laura touched Frank's hand. He had parked and had one leg out of the door. "What is it?"

"Amanda. She doesn't sound right. She told me to read a text she sent me." Laura found the message and clicked. *Reporter Lady in church parking lot asking about lottery winner! We need to do something!*

Laura's head shot up and she combed the parking lot, her eyes darting from row to row. "That reporter is here. Amanda said she's in the parking lot. We've got to stop her."

"How?"

"I don't know yet. Drive around to the other side, she must have moved to the back side of the church."

Frank complied. They both quickly scanned the back parking lot with no sign of Robyn Rogue. "Amanda didn't say which parking lot, maybe the lady's inside already."

Frank parked a second time and they headed for the door.

Amanda had already made it to her seat, but never actually saw Robyn. After she thought about it, she really didn't want to see her and wasn't sure what she would have done had they crossed paths. She was concerned that Robyn might recognize her from the gas station. It wouldn't mean anything necessarily, but Amanda didn't want to take the chance of her eyes giving her away. She felt reporters had special training to read body language and she knew she wasn't good at hiding her emotions at all. Craig asked her with his eyes but all she could do in Joshua's presence, was give a slight head nod of no.

Robyn had made it into the foyer and knew she had to be more discreet. She couldn't zig zag around like in the parking lot, she had to be more careful and study people's reaction to seeing her before approaching with a question. Then she heard it, the voice in her inbox at the station. She moved around others to get closer to it.

Unbeknownst to Robyn, Laura had spotted her and walked right past her, to get to the sanctuary and alerted one of the ushers, who in turn told one of the deacons, that a news reporter was hounding people, the same one who had run a news story on the church that very week. Deacon Johnson overheard the conversation and pulled Deacon Williams to the side. "I bet it's that same lady that was here Wednesday. I'm not gonna bother the pastor with this. She needs to go. She's causing a distraction and stirring up the members. Come with me."

In the foyer, Robyn had pinpointed where the sound was coming from and headed toward the area where she would confront the woman who sent in the tip. It was one of two ladies talking to each other, but their backs were turned. She made two big strides in their direction, then someone grabbed her arm. She turned around to face Deacon Johnson and Deacon Williams who had scowls on their faces.

"Miss, we're going to have to ask you to leave."

"For what?"

"You know why ma'am."

"So, you're telling me I'm not welcome to come to your church?" Robyn reached to secretly turn her recorder on.

"Everyone is welcome but you're here for the wrong reasons. We've gotten a complaint—"

"A complaint?" Her voice rose and Deacon Williams touched her free elbow and guided her out the door while Sister Evella and the lady she was talking to looked on. Evella whispered, "That's Robyn Rogue of Eyewitness News. I wonder why she's here."

While Robyn was being escorted out of the building, she winked at Brent, who walked past her, undetected.

"You can let go of me."

"Miss, we're going to escort you to your car and make sure you leave."

"No. I'm going. Here, at least give your pastor my card. Let him know I am very persistent, and I *will* do a story, with or without him so it would be better for him if he gave his side of the story."

Deacon Johnson took the card, "Have a good day ma'am."

"Oh, I will."

She opened the already-unlocked car and took the keys out from under the floor mat and drove off. She pulled up to the nearest gas station and parked. She quickly got her cell phone out and texted Brent, *record the pastor when he starts talking. I'll pick you up one block from the church. I may have enough to get him to talk to me, but we'll see what he says during this church service.*

Brent was strategic in his seat choice. He needed to be close enough to get a good picture quality from the small hidden camera and be able to pick up a good sound. He pressed record on the video camera in his shirt pocket just for practice. He wanted to make sure he would be able to repeat it with ease when the time came.

Before the Pastor emerged from his office, he was informed of what had happened with the infamous reporter, Robyn Rogue. The church was already a buzz before the pastor could reach the platform. People were whispering and getting distracted by it all.

Pastor sat through two songs by the choir and debated whether to wait until after his sermon to address the situation, which could be done during the announcements. During the third song, he looked over the congregation and felt an uneasiness. He sensed a spirit of confusion quenching Holy Spirit. There were some in the congregation who seemed to be praising God as usual, but there were too many others who were reserved, like they were waiting for something to happen. Then Pastor noticed a visitor fidgeting in his seat. Pastor David glared at him for a moment and caught himself. He didn't know why he was focused on a face he had never seen before. He tried to remember if he truly had met the man, but his memory failed him. He asked God why He would point him out to him, but no answer came. He also felt he was being watched, not just any regular watch but someone staring at him, and he was pulled to look in that direction. He then noticed Sis. Evella seated near the back of the sanctuary. She normally sat near the front. She made sure he noticed her roll her eyes before she turned her gaze while lifting her chin. She was obviously still put off by their meeting. Pastor closed his eyes, he really needed to focus, but he had too much on his mind. He was going to stand in front of the podium in less than fifteen minutes and bring forth a sermon, but he too had been distracted by the morning's events. Even though he didn't witness it firsthand, the details rattled off by his leaders were concerning enough. He wondered if his deacons had handled the situation with the reporter in the right way. They were right not to involve him in matters with the media on a Sunday morning, especially when he had already had a run in with the reporter. And he had recently held a meeting with his staff encouraging them to take on more responsibility so that he could preach and teach more effectively. He also assured them not to be overly concerned with making mistakes, but to just make decisions in love, as Jesus would do, and for the good of the church body. He was sure if they used that to govern their decisions, they could handle almost any issue. But this was no ordinary problem and he hoped he hadn't implemented those changes too soon, because a TV reporter was never on his radar.

He heard the choir finishing up a song and decided to address the situation right way. He got the minister of music's attention before he segued into the final song before the sermon. Pastor David stood and walked to the podium. He looked around the room and glanced up into the balcony. He started tapping his finger on the top of the podium then he grabbed both sides of it, as if he were holding himself up. Brent swallowed hard, reached inside his jacket, and pushed record.

"Brothers and Sisters, I feel the need to address a situation that took place this morning. I want you to hear it from me firsthand, so those who've been whispering can stop already." Pastor addressed everyone calmly but you could see the disappointment in his eyes and his voice matched it. "And after I address it, it doesn't have to be talked about anymore, right? We can go on and have service like we know we should."

"That's right, Pastor."

"Isn't that the truth."

The comments rang out.

"I know some of you have seen the news footage because you've come up and told me. For those of you who haven't, I'll bring you up to speed. Two stories were done, the first one about the gas station on the corner where someone won the lottery last year, or maybe it was two years ago, I don't remember. But I don't remember what I had to eat last week either. I know I'm not the only one."

That comment was met with giggles throughout the congregation.

"So why are they talking about it now? Because the new Texas law just passed that says you can remain anonymous if you win, but the person who won last year, or two years ago, found another way to remain unknown before the law was even passed. Despite that, the media is trying to find out who they are. That leads us to the second news story. For some reason, they think that the winner is associated with this church. Now why would they think that? I'll let you ponder that on your own. But let me tell you this. If you play the lottery and win, this is one church that will accept it. If you go up the road to Coushatta and win on red 27 bring it on, just don't gamble your tithe money."

"Amen," someone shouted.

"Or your rent money; everything in moderation. If one of you win playing crips—"

"It's craps," someone yelled.

"Hey, there you go. Uh huh, I know what it is, I just got tired of y'all looking at me like you don't know what I'm talking about. Don't play with me; I've been living a long time."

Laughter gushed out like a wave, sweeping over the room.

"And you know what happens when you throw a rock in a pack of dogs. The one who hollers, is the one it hit." He looked at a man in the middle of one of the rows. "Thank you for being real brother. No shame in that. Own it."

A few claps erupted throughout the church.

"I'm glad it wasn't one of the ministers or deacons who yelled it out; not because there's anything wrong with it, it's just because some of you couldn't take it. You'd talk about them like a dog when you secretly do it yourselves. Lord, deliver me from hypocrites."

"Oooh, go 'head Pastor."

"You said a mouthful."

"Teach us." The comments surfaced like popcorn being popped in the microwave; so fast and overlapping, you can't hear the two-second silence your ear is straining to detect.

"Are y'all afraid of what I'm gonna say if I find out you gamble? That's not a sin and even if it was, I don't have a heaven or hell to put you in." Pastor David took a deep breath. "I didn't even mean to say all that."

"That's alright Pastor, we must have needed to hear it." An elderly lady who sat near the front belted out.

"Alright," David smiled. "I'll take it."

"Now what happened today is, a news reporter was here at the church apparently asking several of you questions about it. The same lady came Wednesday night right before Bible Study, trying to talk to me about it. Now you all know how I operate. There's a time and place for anything, and everything should be done decent and in order, so she was asked to leave. You know I don't want our church to be made out of a circus. I won't be pressured into talking to a reporter and I don't want you to be either. Before you ask me, I'll tell you now, I don't know if I'll talk to her or not, because I don't like what I've seen on the news thus far. So, I hope that clears everything up. If you have any concerns come see me, but please don't go around gossiping and spreading rumors. If someone asks why this happened or why that happened, don't feed into that just say, 'hold on let's call the pastor right now and ask him.' I bet you that'll squash it."

"I know that's right," a congregant shouted.

"Now, can we have church?" The applause and chants gave the answer.

Pastor David returned to his seat while the choir director got back in position and the minister of music struck the chords.

Brent figured nothing else of relevance would be said so he stopped the recording. He pondered leaving but knew that would be too obvious. He would have to stay until the end of service unless he saw the window of opportunity he needed, a number of people leaving at one time, but that was unlikely. He shot Robyn a text message stating he had gotten some footage and she replied with a thumbs-up emoji.

He felt uneasy the entire time, especially when he didn't stand up when they called for visitors. He was sure people noticed that he wasn't a regular attendee, but he didn't want to call any attention to himself either. He also second-guessed making a bee-line toward the door immediately after what they called their fellowship period. How would it look, him leaving right after exchanging so many handshakes and hugs from strangers full of smiles?

The service continued with the pastor eventually returning to the podium and preaching a sermon titled, *If you dig one ditch, you'd better dig two,* which the pastor subtitled, *If you plan to dig a ditch for me, you'd better dig one for you,* the lesson of which made Brent uneasy, yet he couldn't leave in the middle of the pastor preaching; that would be rude. Brent studied the program in his hand, reading each line, planning how he could escape. The sermon would be followed by the Invitation, Offering and Announcements, and finally the Benediction.

He started to leave during the Invitation but the screen above the choir said 'please don't move unless you're responding to the Invitation' so he sat there, handcuffed to his seat by obedience, or maybe just the idea of not breaking any customs. The offering was his best shot but when it was time for that, instead of having each row of people walk to the front, baskets were passed down each aisle so he couldn't just get up. And if he would have left without putting some type of money into the basket, he felt people would look down on him.

Ushers lined the aisles in preparation for the offering. He peeked inside his wallet and forced his eyes shut, regretting the missed opportunity of stopping by the corner store to get some change. He searched both pants pockets but only felt lint, so he returned his hand to his wallet, retrieved a ten-dollar bill, and surrendered it to the red velvet-lined basket. Finally, the announcements were next. All previous attempts to leave seemed too awkward, but this may be a safe time. This was his chance to escape, but before he could get his leg up, the pastor said "Now I understand if some of you have to leave to go to work but if not, stay. You don't want to miss the departing blessing." Without moving his head, Brent's eyes tested the power of his peripheral vision. He looked to the far left and right to see if there were any takers, but no one else moved. He surely couldn't look behind him, which would have sent the wrong signal, so he closed his eyes, sighed, and waited until the end of service.

Brent finally made his way to the exit after service was dismissed. And now, as he headed out the door, he still felt a little uneasy, but he pushed those feelings aside in exchange of the euphoria he felt being undercover and capturing the pastor on tape.

Pastor called a meeting after service and had the deacons round up the other leaders to come to his office. He hardly waited for the door to close before starting. "Now I said I didn't want our church to be a circus, all in the media. I don't know if this happened because I talked about the donation over the pulpit last year or not, if so, that's my fault. People want to know what's going on in their church, but I guess I'm gonna have to keep some stuff to myself, or just tell my 'Peter, James, and John folk,' do I have any bible readers in here?"

"Go ahead pastor," someone muttered.

"Do what you need to do, we understand," Deacon Johnson nodded.

"Well, I don't care where the money came from, it is a blessing. Money is not good or bad, if it's in my hand it's blessed money if it's in a drug dealer's hand it's cursed money, it all depends on what it's used for."

Heads nodded.

"I just want y'all to know that I stand behind the decision that was made today to escort the reporter off the premises. I'll pray about how to handle this whole thing and take it from there. Y'all enjoy the rest of your Sunday."

Someone opened the door and the crowd dispersed. Meanwhile, Brent had already met back up with Robyn, who was eager to see what she could use from the tape. And he was still on a high from being able to pull it all off.

C22

CRAIG'S PHONE RANG with the new song he'd picked out for Joshua's mom, Fred Hammond's *No Weapon.* The lyrics reminded him that no matter what evil plot his ex had planned against him, it would not prosper. He didn't feel like answering but he also didn't want her to retaliate by dissuading Josh from spending time with his family, so Craig appeased and picked up the call.

"So, I heard someone at your church won the lottery."

Craig stopped dead in his tracks. The lump in his throat almost made him gag but he had to play it cool. He couldn't deny it because she obviously heard it from somewhere, but he couldn't bring any attention on himself by responding defensively.

"That's just a rumor."

"How is it just a rumor when a reporter came up to Josh and asked him about it?"

Craig closed his eyes. *So that's how she found out, of course,* he thought. He couldn't blame his son for saying something. He and Amanda didn't tell him not to say anything because that would be suspicious. *If Josh knew he'd probably tell Gloria, even if I told him not to. He's hot-headed and is more loyal to her than me anyway. I need to downplay this,* he thought. "I don't know Gloria, why don't you call the reporter and ask her, I don't care."

"Uh huh."

He could feel her wheels turning.

"Was it you?"

"Was it me, what?" He tried to sound indifferent.

"Did you win the lottery?"

"If I did, I certainly wouldn't tell you. Is that all you called for?"

"I notice you didn't answer the question."

"Oh, my God," He exhaled loudly. "No…Gloria…I did not win the lottery." *Lord, I didn't win, we did. So, I'm not even lying,* he pleaded with God. He would have said "no" regardless if it was the truth or not, he would've just had to ask God for forgiveness later. Right now, he just needed to get her off the phone before he said the wrong thing. He needed to think this through at a later date, as far as all the curve balls she may come up with. But the most important thing he needed to do right now was to think fast. "Don't call me with foolishness." He thought maybe that slight insult would get her off the phone.

"Let me guess…you've got to go because you have something to do."

"No, I have absolutely nothing to do, but I don't want to talk to you. Bye." He hung up before she could grill him further. She had talked to him much worse over the years, so he felt justified in his response now, and it was for a much greater cause. No matter what happened,

Gloria was the last person on earth that could ever find out about this win.

Craig found the nearest chair and let his body drop. His heart raced. *What if she finds out? Would she be able to get my money?* Their lawyer had assured him and Amanda of the unlikeliness that Gloria would ever know they won but even if she found out, she had no legal claim to any of it. It all sounded good, but this recent phone call had him doubting. Craig needed assurance so he dialed the number that went straight to their lawyer's cell phone. Not everyone in the pool was convinced to keep Mr. Roberts on a hefty retainer to get more access to him, but Craig was one who certainly realized the benefit, now more than ever.

"Hello Craig. What can I do for you?"

The salutation shouldn't have surprised Craig, since their lawyer was personable, but knowing Mr. Roberts had saved Craig's number in his personal cell phone was impressive. "Hi Mr. Roberts. Look I just got a call from my ex. My son told her about a reporter coming to the church and asking about a lottery winner. Anyway, she asked me if I won. Of course, I told her "no," but I want to make sure she can't get anything, even if she does find out."

"Take a deep breath. I can tell she rattled you. The answer is "no." She's not entitled to any portion of the money you won, but—"

"But? What but!"

"I was just going to talk about the child support part."

"What part? I paid off all the back child support I owed. You said—"

"Yes, yes. And when we paid off the arrears and the little that was left for the scheduled payments, the account was paid in full, so you're fine. All I was going to say is that if she would have informed the courts that your son was continuing his education, the child support payments would have continued. But you had already told me that she wasn't trying to help him go to college, so I didn't bring it up."

"But he is going to college. I'm paying for him to go."

"She must not know that child support stipulation or she would probably press the issue and get the support extended."

"She can't if I'm paying for his college, right?"

"That's up to the judge's discretion. Paying your arrears was a pretty big lump sum. She might have just been so happy to get that all at once she didn't think about anything else. Maybe she just let you slide with that. Consider yourself lucky."

"No, not her. If she had a gallon of water and I had a thimble full, she'd want the water in my thimble too, just so I wouldn't have anything. She didn't let me slide; she just didn't know. Lord, I hope it stays that way. And Mr. Roberts, there's no such thing as luck. I'm not lucky, I'm blessed."

"That's an interesting statement, especially coming from a lottery winner."

"Playing a game based on chance, I get it. That's what the world says. But I know my life is guided by God and not some superficial force called luck."

"Point taken. Rest assured, she can't get any money from you. She's not entitled to one red cent."

"That's all I wanted to know. I appreciate you." Craig hung up and let out a sigh of relief.

***

Pastor David and his wife sat in front of the television to look at the recorded newscast from the bible study night, when he refused to speak with the reporter, Robyn. He had wanted to avoid watching it, but the escalation of Sunday's events forced him to. They watched the negative news report which ended with "I tried to contact His Way Church for comment, but the church did not respond."

Pastor David kept repeating that phrase over and over in his mind. It just didn't set well with him. Even though he nor the church did anything wrong, the news report still cast them in a negative light. And the church's non-response comment added fuel to the insult. He contemplated what else the reporter could conjure up, especially since she had been escorted out Sunday. Her next report could be even worse. Loretta interrupted his thoughts with a question.

"Do you think it was the lottery?"

"What's that?"

"The donation; I've been hearing things and wondered if it's true."

"I don't know." He shook his head slowly. "I really don't know." He paused. "Do you think I should do this interview?"

"For what purpose?"

"To set the record straight."

"But you don't know where the donation came from."

"No, I'm talking about clearing up this nonsense about the church not having a response."

Loretta's eyebrows lowered.

"I'm not talking about our church per se, I'm talking about The Church. The Church always has a response, an answer to any life situation. I may can shed some light on the lottery, or gambling in general. People need to hear that it's not a sin, and they shouldn't be condemned for it. And I'm sure some pastors are saying otherwise because me and Pastor Anthony have different views on it."

"How is someone from the outside looking in going to understand what's right and wrong if pastors can't even agree on it?"

He threw up his hands. "My point exactly. This same thing has been going on since Jesus walked the earth. That's one of the reasons why Christianity is not drawing people, we in leadership are still separated on simple ideas, just like the Pharisees and Sadducees were. Sometimes we take our personal hang-ups and make that the litmus test of what's right and wrong for Christians, but we can't do that. That's one of the reasons why Christianity isn't attractive to the world. I want to point out that people need to read The Word for themselves and don't just take a minister's word for it, including me. We're human too and still are subject to error. Don't get me wrong, I am anointed but I'm not perfect."

"I know," Loretta smirked. "Your plan is good, but I want you to beware because reporters can twist your words or edit out things and downright delete relevant things you say and just focus on one thing to prove whatever point they're trying to make."

"I know, but I can't *not* say something."

"I'll be praying about it."

"I already knew that." He leaned over and gave her a kiss then took out his wallet and retrieved Robyn Rogue's business card.

C23

THE CHURCH POOL decided to get together to go over different scenarios and roll play in case the meddling reporter showed up again, at church or anywhere else; and to prepare them for questions from anyone unexpected. Frank and Laura were in the kitchen preparing hors d'oeuvres before their company showed up. They stood beside each other rinsing and cutting up fruits and vegetables. Laura started chopping the carrots harder than necessary. She chopped faster, forcing the knife down, making grooves into the cutting board. Frank reached over and grabbed the hand that held the knife.

"What's wrong?"

"This is all my fault," Laura let the knife fall.

"What is?"

"If I hadn't bought the ticket so close to the church, we wouldn't be going through this right now."

"Why didn't you say something earlier? I mean, I don't know what difference it would have made but maybe we would have been better prepared."

"I don't know. Embarrassed? I mean, what are the odds that the one time I buy tickets at the closest gas station near the church, would be the time we would win?" She shook her head.

"What happened that day? Why did you wait till the last minute to buy them, I thought you usually do it on your lunch break?"

"I had a working lunch that day, some deadline I was working on. And I got off late too. I was trying to get to bible study on time. I passed up the spot I normally go because the parking lot was full, and I meant to stop somewhere else, but I lost too much time sitting in traffic. I remember it like it was yesterday because there was an overturned 18-wheeler. It wasn't even on my side of traffic. It was on the other side of the freeway, but everybody on my side was looking at the accident."

"Rubbernecking," Frank blurted out as a crevice appeared between his eyebrows. "Why do people do that, that's what I don't understand? Help me understand that. You're not going to help so why even look that way, why slow down? It's like you just wanna see somebody dead. You caused all that traffic just because you want to be nosey and you're not going to do a doggone thing."

Laura looked at her husband. "Can I continue with my story?"

A smile peaked from the corner of Frank's mouth. "I don't think it's a big deal."

"Well, we'll see what the others have to say about it."

As if her words had summoned the others, the doorbell rang.

Frank left the kitchen, while Laura opened the dip and placed it in the middle of the platter.

Some small talk occurred until all the members were there, and Amanda got Jorge and Maria on her cellphone so they could get everyone's input.

Laura started. "OK everyone. Let's just address the elephant in the room first. After the first newscast, which lovely Amanda here starred as an extra..." Amanda rolled her eyes, and everyone laughed. "...you all found out that I bought the tickets at the closest gas station near the church, a place I said I wasn't going to buy them at. I truly apologize for that. It's a long story but I still should have gone somewhere else and just been late to church that night. None of us want the publicity that our church is now facing so if you want to blame me, I deserve it."

A few broke their gaze or didn't look up at all. The silence was deafening. Frank squeezed Laura's shoulder.

Don's face contorted. "No, this is a good reminder of what could have happened...no, what would have happened, if we didn't stay anonymous. This is a walk in the park compared to what we would be going through if we hadn't set up the blind trust. We can never repay you for that."

Heads nodded and Laura took in a deep breath and exhaled.

"Besides, we wouldn't have ever won if you hadn't have gone there. If you would have went to another store, then that store would not have had those set of numbers." Jorge's voice broke through the speaker on the phone.

Laura felt her throat tighten so she swallowed. Her heartbeat grew louder. She looked up at Frank, who discreetly nodded his head and warned her with his eyes, to keep quiet and just agree with Jorge's statement.

Craig interrupted. "I have no room to talk in this discussion after what we did. There's nothing we have to say. We're just happy to be part of it."

Maria said, "No, hold on a minute. I thought we were over that. We decided to include you guys. It's a done deal with that so don't even bring it up anymore. We're all partners in this and you have an equal voice."

Craig nodded in surrender.

"We do have a bit of a situation," Amanda glanced at Craig, urging him to fill everyone in.

"You all know my son, Josh. We're trying to build a relationship with him, so he's been staying with us. Well, the reporter asked him if he knew anything about someone at church winning the lottery, and he mentioned it to his mother, who then called me asking about it."

"How did you handle that?" Don's eyes were glued to Craig.

Craig held up his hands, "I denied it of course but I don't know if she bought it or not. She might snoop around."

"I can guarantee you she will." Amanda added.

Janet turned to Laura. "Is there anything she can do? I mean, can she find out anything?"

"No, everything is iron tight. Mr. Roberts explained all that. The only way someone could find out, is if we tell them."

"Craig, Amanda, you're going to have to be very careful around your son. You're not used to having him around, so it may be easier for you to trip up around him."

Craig and Amanda looked at each other, acknowledging how severe the situation could get if they weren't careful.

"And there's nothing you could have done to prevent this," Tammy offered.

"Tammy's right, any hints or doing anything to stop him from telling his mom would not have been good," Frank removed his hand from Laura's shoulder, grateful the attention had moved elsewhere.

"Let's just make sure we stay focused and be more aware and maybe think of some responses, just in case someone at church, or that Robyn woman, asks us something," Janet offered.

"And we may all want to avoid going to that gas station for a while." Amanda warned.

"No problemo here," Maria joked, "Maybe you all come visit here."

"Maybe after the smoke clears," Frank leaned over to make sure his voice was heard through the phone.

"OK, we will hold you to it," Jorge agreed.

The phone conversation ended, and they did a few role-playing exercises anticipating questions and practicing their answers. They all agreed to be even more vigilant and hoped the situation would work itself out.

***

"So, you chose UofH, huh? I'm proud of you." Craig rubbed his son's head while he still brandished the red baseball cap that spelled out *Cougars*. "You're going to do great things. Just stay focused. Listen, I know you've been complaining to your mother because you think because I'm paying for school, that I'm trying to control you. Yes, I want to know what your degree is and insist you work while you get it but son, that builds character. It will make you set priorities. I'm trying to teach you something. I didn't raise you and I see I've got to correct some things. I've got to teach you how to be a man, and I don't have long to do it. I've got a really short time. Your mom had you for eighteen years; what do I have about four, six at the most? I've lived this life and I'm trying to get you prepared. I thought I knew everything when I was in my twenties and still didn't know what I didn't know. I just want you to listen because, I've been there. I want you to be better than I was, and to do better than I did."

"But Dad it's hard to work and go to school."

"Son, that's the problem; nobody's been hard on you enough. You gotta man up. You can do it, just don't let the girls distract you. Be careful who you choose. I hope you keep yourself pure and don't sleep with anyone. You may think you know what you want, but you really don't know what you're doing. There are a lot of good women out there, but there are a whole bunch of women that prey on men too, just to get a steady check for eighteen years. Keep your pants zipped up and respect the young ladies because that's not what college is about. You're there to learn."

Josh rolled his eyes. "I know Dad, I know. And how are you all of a sudden able to pay for my college 'for as many degrees as I want to get', to use your words?"

"This new job was a blessing and I get bonuses." He searched his son's face for any hint that Gloria's skepticism had gotten to him. "And I'm not giving it all away paying child support." Craig jabbed his son's ribs. A playful gesture but Craig really wanted to get Josh's mind on something else. He hoped that his son wasn't starting to get suspicious.

C24

ROBYN WAS SILENT, focusing on every detail of the footage being replayed on the flat screen in her office. This was the first look at the footage Brent took on Sunday. She squinted her eyes and tilted her head, rewinding parts to listen for ways she could use any snippets to craft her story. She resembled a lion on the prowl, waiting for the right opportunity to pounce on his prey.

"Robyn, I don't see anything wrong with anything he said."

"Shhhh, I think I can use this to—"

"Why are you doing this?" Brent interrupted.

Robyn adjusted her posture.

"What are you trying to prove?" Brent tried again.

"The public has a right to know."

"No, they don't. If the winner wants to stay out of the news, let them. If they want to give this church some money, let 'em. Why bother this pastor?"

She shrugged her shoulders. "I don't know; it's a challenge. Aren't you fascinated? Let's see if the winner slipped up." She pressed rewind again. "I don't have anything against the pastor. He just happens to be a victim of circumstance."

"I think you're trying to make a name for yourself, but there're more important stories we could be covering."

"That's the point. Viewers get tired of the same story every day; murder, crime, theft, embezzlement. They want a different story, something to keep them engaged. Everyone likes a good lotto story because everyone wants to win, but a lot of people are ashamed to even say they play. That's what makes this so interesting. You know how many calls I've gotten since I did the report in front of the church?"

"What kind of calls, what did they say?"

"Some of them were bad mouthing any church that approved of gambling. Some told me to leave the church alone. But hey, it got attention, much more attention than the regular stories we air. That's the point; engagement. Increase engagement, increase ratings."

Brent shook his head.

"But you're right there's not much here, but I can use some of what I got when they threw me out."

"You were taping?"

"Of course, I was. A reporter is always prepared. You never know what you can use."

Her phone buzzed and she reached into her pocket to retrieve it. She swiped a few times and read the screen. "My my, did you know that same church had that big building added on last year?"

"So?"

"They paid in cash. Now, Brent, tell me, why would they build a new building, and pay cash for it when they still owe on the current building?"

"How do you know all that?"

"I've got my ways. You can find out pretty much anything if you know who to ask."

Her phone rang. "Robyn Rogue speaking. Oh, hello Pastor Wright. Thank you for calling." She turned to Brent, whose mouth fell open.

Robyn scurried over to her desk and picked up a pen and pad and scribbled some notes down. She shook her head. "No hard feelings, just doing my job…yes, set the record straight, I agree. The public wants to hear what a pastor like you has to say about it." She glared at Brent. "Tomorrow will be perfect. See you then."

"You've got to be kidding."

"Yes! I got it. I interview him tomorrow morning. Strategy Brent, pure strategy. He may not have admitted to anything during church service, but I'll trip him up in the interview."

Brent closed his eyes and pinched his lips together.

"Well, this has been a productive day."

"So, I guess you're gonna prepare some questions for him?"

"Already done, *he'd* better be prepared for *me*."

***

"How did your mom's appointment go?" Laura joined Frank at the kitchen table.

Frank's hand trembled as he put it up to his face. "She has cancer."

"Oh my God, Frank, I'm sorry; Lord Jesus help."

Frank cleared his throat to gain his composure. "She hasn't been taking all of her medicines either because she says she can't afford it."

"What about insurance?"

"It doesn't cover everything. And she refused some treatment the doctor suggested because of what she would have to pay out of pocket. I told the doctor, right in front of her, to do whatever he needs to do, and I'll take care of it. I told her not to even look at the bills, just put them in a pile on the counter and I'll pick them up when I come over. I don't want her to be stressing over anything. I just want her to concentrate on getting well."

"That's good Frank. I'm so glad you let her know, so she won't have to worry. What did the doctor say?"

"*He* didn't say much, it was my mamma doing most of the talking about that. She told me that wasn't necessary, and she didn't want us spending our money on her. I told her we have money saved up in money market accounts, retirement, and such." He shook his head. "I don't get it. When I finally convinced her to show me some of the bills, yeah, it's a lot for someone on a fixed income, but she seems like she's just given up."

"She probably doesn't think she has anything to live for." Laura looked intently in Frank's eyes and hoped he could read between the lines. His tears gave the answer. "I think you can change that. Just you being there can give her something to fight for."

Frank shook his head in agreement. He already knew what he had to do, and he wasn't going to waste any more precious time.

C25

ROBYN WALKED INTO the sanctuary of His Way Church and observed everything, looking around like she was touring a museum. Deacons Johnson and Williams, one in front and one behind, escorted her and Brent to the pastor's office where he was waiting. The men were cordial but reserved. Robyn nor Brent asked them anything, and the deacons didn't volunteer any information. They too had seen the news story and didn't want to say anything that could be used against them or the church. The safest thing to do in their minds was to remain silent.

Once inside Pastor Wright's office, Brent set up the video equipment as Robyn and Pastor Wright exchanged small talk. The two deacons sat quietly with watchful eyes.

"Sir, I'm going to ask that you remove your hat, please." Pastor directed to Brent, who was wearing a baseball cap so low you could barely make out his eyes.

Brent removed it. He and Pastor Wright's eyes met, and Brent knew Pastor Wright recognized him as the same new face in the crowd that Sunday morning.

Pastor Wright cupped his hands and leaned back in his chair. Brent quickly turned away to look like he was busy with the final touches of his preparation, but he was so good and fast at his job, he could do it in his sleep. Meanwhile, Pastor Wright thought about canceling the interview altogether; the deception was a bit much for him to handle.

"Brent, are we ready to tape?"

"Ready."

Robyn nodded at the pastor then looked at the camera. "If you've been following my features on *In Our Own Backyard*, you've heard me talk about House Bill 59 that was passed, which now allows Texas lottery winners who win one million dollars or more to remain anonymous. There has been some speculation, since the winning ticket was purchased at a convenience store down the street, that some of the winnings landed right here at this church. I have Pastor David Wright of His Way Church located right here in North Houston. Thank you, Pastor for agreeing to meet with me."

He chuckled. "I really didn't want to, but you caused quite a stir at our church with your other TV reports and your presence here on Sunday morning." He figured he'd get that out in the open first in case she tried to use that against him later.

"And why didn't you want to meet with me in the first place?"

"I have a job to do. I'm about making sure souls get saved and teaching people how to live Godly lives. I know the saying about any publicity is good publicity, but I don't want your viewers to come to our church because they think a lottery winner is here. That's coming for the wrong reason."

"Is there a lottery winner at your church?"

"I don't know. Just because we're the closest church to the gas station doesn't mean anything?"

"You're right but what does it mean when you build a youth center right around the time that there's a ten-million-dollar lottery win? And I got a tip that your church received a substantial donation."

"You certainly did your homework. The youth center has been a blessing to the community. Families can bring their children out and be taught God's word on their level while the parents learn in the sanctuary. And yes, we did get a donation, but that's not the first time, nor the last. And I will say that if someone does win the lottery, we will gladly accept that donation."

"So, you don't see anything wrong with gambling?"

"It's really not important what I think is right or wrong, but what the bible has to say about it. And I don't see anywhere in the bible where it's wrong to do so. There is a warning about chasing fantasies, which the lottery and any gambling could be considered, but it is not a sin. Everything in moderation."

"I've heard about a pastor that wouldn't accept a lottery gift. Why is that?"

"Well, I don't know his reasoning, we have our own convictions, I guess. Maybe he didn't want all the negative attention, like our church is getting now with just the speculation. And I can see why a winner wouldn't want the whole world to know. I support this new bill."

"Some would disagree with that. And from inception lotteries revealed the names of the winners to ensure the public's trust of the lottery system itself."

"Ms. Rogue, we've come a long way in this society. State and federal lotteries are reputable, and most people don't question the validity of the system itself. And I believe we should protect the winners by allowing them to enjoy their money without fear, intimidation, or unsolicited attention."

"I beg to differ, Pastor Wright. When someone plays the lottery, they already know the expectation if they win, their information will be public."

"And that needs to change. You are one in a few, I would imagine, who have a problem with not knowing, and maybe that's because of the profession you're in, but some things need to be left unknown."

"On the contrary, Pastor. There's only a handful of states that allow anonymity, the majority do not because they know how important it is for each lottery, small or large, to be able to show their patrons actual real people are winning their particular lottery, which is why they take pictures of the person, and give out their information."

"Well, I am glad that we have forward thinking leaders in Texas because both the Senate and the House passed the bill unanimously, so they agree as I do that we should honor the wishes of those winners who want to stay out of the limelight."

Robyn blinked rapidly and Brent lifted his eyebrows. She wasn't the only one who had done their homework.

"Is your church going to give ten percent of your *donation* to a charity like it teaches its members to do?"

Why would she ask me something like that? "That is an interesting question, and an assumption. No—"

"Your *answer* is more interesting. Let me get this straight. You preach what the bible says right?"

"Yes."

"So, the bible says to give ten percent. You call it tithing. So, if your members give the church ten percent, why doesn't the church give ten percent?"

Pastor Wright squinted his eyebrows and took a long look at Robyn. *This lady is on an ego trip. She's still upset that I wouldn't see her, and she was asked to leave. She's trying to make this personal.* "You didn't let me finish. No, we don't give ten percent, we give about ninety percent."

Before she realized it, she had let out an audible gasp.

"Ms. Rogue, we are not a for-profit business, we are a non-profit. We give the money back in many different ways. We give to missions work in other countries to help build wells so families will have access to clean water, build schools, fund churches, and provide medical supplies. And of course, we help here at home, especially in our own community. We have all types of outreach and activities at the church; like health fairs, school supply drives, and our prison ministry which includes an angel tree where we buy toys and give care packages to households with children who have a parent incarcerated. It takes money to have teaching materials, snacks for children, because some parents don't feed them before coming, you name it. Churches also have light bills, mortgages, water, and many other expenses, just like the average person. Churches are the backbone of society. We do more than some people realize."

"Thank you, Pastor Wright. And I'm sure your donation will help with all of that. Well, you've heard it here on *In Our Own Backyard.*"

Brent held up three fingers and counted down to zero by taking each finger away, one by one. "And you're clear."

Robyn jumped out of her seat and thanked Pastor Wright for the interview. The two deacons popped up as well, ready to escort their visitors to the parking lot.

"Will this air today?" Pastor Wright held out his hand to shake hers.

"I'll have to see. It depends on how much editing needs to be done."

"I see." His thoughts went back to the conversation he had with his wife. "Ms. Rogue, I expect it to be true and represent our conversation accurately, no cutting and pasting to make it seem like I'm saying something I'm not."

"Of course. I'll be in touch."

"Thank you, Ms. Rogue. You're very good at what you do." Pastor Wright thought maybe his kindness would soften her vendetta against him and convince her to do the right thing regarding the footage.

"Well, thank you, and thank you for your time." Robyn accepted the complement without displaying any emotion. She was experienced enough to know that emotion was a liability in her line of work. It dulled the senses and took away the ability to be objective on a story. She had to remain removed from the story enough to expose anything and anyone that needed it. And a pastor or a church was no exception. She turned around and walked out the door.

C26

PASTOR DAVID SAT in his chair in the quiet living room. His body slumped over, elbows on the armrests, his head held up by his hands as if he were praying, but he was in deep thought. The interview with Robyn Rogue weighed heavy on his mind. He now doubted whether he should have done the interview, after all he had nothing to prove. He felt he may have risked too much, giving in to her pressures of having the interview in the first place. She could cut and slice their interview to make it say whatever she wanted. He shook his head, wanting to chastise himself for trusting a reporter. He also second guessed himself for not calling out the fact that her camera man had been in the church service, blending in with his congregation. *Lord, why didn't I say something? I should have canceled the interview right then.* He tried desperately to remember if he had said anything in the pulpit that could be turned into something negative in a news report, for he was positive that was the only reason the camera man had been there.

His phone rang and with one glance at the screen, he dropped his head. Pastor Anthony was the last person he wanted to talk to. He had either heard something or was about to point something out on the news stories that had already aired. As bad as he wanted to ignore the call, he wanted to get his mind off of questioning himself over the interview with the reporter, so he answered.

"Hello, Pastor Anthony."

"You don't sound too good my brother. Are you OK?"

Pastor David sat up to make his voice come alive. "Yes, yes, I've just got a lot on my mind, but I'm fine. What can I do for you?"

"I was just calling to check on you. I heard you had an interview with that news reporter. What's her name?"

"Robyn Rogue."

"Ah, yes, that's it. Well, how did it go?"

Pastor David rolled his eyes. "I don't know. I made my point, but we'll see how they spin it."

"Hmmm."

"And how did you know about the interview anyway?"

"You told Pastor Keith to pray for you, and he asked me to pray for you too. When I asked him what specifically to pray about, he told me about the interview."

Pastor David looked at the ceiling. He wanted to ask God why He had such a sense of humor at a time like this. The irony of Pastor Anthony praying for him when he knew they disagreed vehemently on the morality of playing the lottery was too much to take in at the moment. He would no doubt gloat in whatever peril may come out of the airing of this interview. His self-righteousness would be unbearable.

There was a thump at the door, so Pastor David turned to make sure he had actually heard the noise. Then keys rattled. He smiled and headed for the door, grateful for the chance to end the conversation. "Uh, Pastor Anthony, I've gotta go."

"So soon?"

"Yes, I'm afraid so." He opened the door and grabbed the bags slipping from his wife's hands. "My wife needs help with the groceries." He gave a quick bye and smacked a kiss on Loretta's cheek. "Girl, you have perfect timing."

She smiled. "And so do you." She peeled off the post-it note she had been unsuccessfully reaching for. "Honey, you didn't hear the doorbell ring?"

"Nobody rang the doorbell."

"Well, you missed a delivery." She handed him the note that read, *third and final notice,* stamped in red. The header read *FedEx.*

C27

PASTOR DAVID'S CELL phone rang but at first glance he didn't recognize the number. He picked up anyway.

"Pastor David, this is Brent, the camera man with Eyewitness News. I'm calling to inform you that your interview will air this afternoon at the six o'clock newscast time."

"O.K. Thank you for calling and letting me know, but I was expecting Ms. Rogue to call me. I wanted to make sure—"

"I'm sorry she couldn't contact you herself, but she wanted to make sure you were aware. And don't worry, you will be pleased."

You will be pleased. How would you know what would be pleasing, Pastor David thought.

Brent hung up without a "bye" or "thanks" or any word that would conclude a normal conversation and David didn't know what to make of it. With a click in his ear, the call ended just as quickly as it had begun. Pastor David looked at his watch. He only had twenty minutes before the news would begin. His stomach felt queasy. He yelled out Loretta's name and sent text messages to the two deacons that had been present during the interview. He also alerted Pastors Keith, Henry, and Anthony; although he wasn't quite sure why. Loretta came in the room and he explained everything to her. They both were glued to the TV.

The *In Our Own Backyard* segment came on towards the end. Pastor David looked at his watch and noted there was fifteen minutes left in the broadcast. He reasoned that was a good sign that perhaps his entire interview would be shown, and not just a smidgen of what the newscast could use for their own agenda. On the other hand, he considered the camera man could have been recording that Sunday morning and they were planning to include that footage however they wished. He imagined the reporter kicking and screaming, putting on a grand performance, as she was being "thrown out of a church," he was sure she would say in her version of events. What a spectacle that would be on the news for the whole city to see. And what recourse would he have against a behemoth of a news station if they got the story all wrong and cast an unfavorable light on him and the church? His Way Church and especially him as the pastor would be a mockery inside and outside of the faith community. Pastor David started rubbing his legs as the intro music to Robyn's segment started.

Robyn Rogue appeared on screen and Pastor David examined her every word. "This interview concludes my three-part story of the anonymous lottery winner…"

Concludes? Rather this turns out good or bad at least this will be over soon, David reasoned.

They both watched the segment in silence, each looking for something different. Loretta looking for her husband and pastor to be strong and confident in his words, and for him not to get tripped up by any traps the reporter may place. Pastor David already knew he did well in the interview so he was watching for any editing tricks that could essentially change his answers to mean something totally different. Loretta squeezed her husband's knee in admiration as she watched and listened to him hold his own.

After it was over, Pastor David sat back, dumbfounded by what he had just witnessed. He had been so concerned about what this reporter could and might do but he had just watched the entire interview exactly how it was actually taped. Nothing added, and nothing taken away. No clips of him talking inside the sanctuary Sunday morning with Brent canvassing his every word, no quotes from church members whom Robyn had painstakingly hunted down in the parking lot, and no footage of her being escorted out of the church building. He couldn't believe it. She could have easily added footage of herself being escorted off of the church grounds, twice, but she hadn't. And tonight, she started the story saying "this concludes" which meant she wouldn't be having any follow-ups. None of this made sense. It was great, but too great to be true, or was he overthinking things again? God had answered his prayers, why doubt that things would work out the way he wanted them to? Wasn't that just like God to step-in right-on time?

"Honey, that was perfect. You did it. I'm so proud of you."

Pastor David started laughing through his big smile, relief resting on him like a warm sunset against his skin. He grabbed Loretta and embraced her.

***

Pastor David returned home from running errands, one of which was to go to the FedEx distribution center and pick up his package as indicated from the post-it note left on his door. He placed the envelope on the coffee table in the living room and sat there silently, just as he had in his car in the parking lot when he placed the large envelope on the passenger's seat several months prior. His mind raced back to the day that changed His Way Church for the better. *Could it be? No, that's silly. Lightening doesn't strike twice in the same spot. Anyway, last time the package was sent to the church. This was sent to my house. Maybe I'm getting worked up about nothing.* All kinds of thoughts claimed his mind. He started biting his hangnails and his foot shook up and down while he sat in his chair, one leg crossed over the other. Loretta was in their bedroom and he needed to find a way to tell her.

It had been over a year and a half ago when he anonymously received Frank and Laura's tithes on their portion of the lottery win. This new envelope contained tithes from the rest of the group, including Jorge and Maria, who finally decided to give their tithes to Pastor David's church, the church they belonged to when they won, even though they had started their own church in Mexico. The package also included a generous love offering to Pastor David himself, the amount larger than some people's retirement fund.

Pastor David let out a deep breath and found Loretta. He brought her back into the living room, and sat her on the sofa. "Loretta, I have something to tell you. You can't share this with anyone else."

"OK," she turned her head slightly.

"The donation we received at the church over a year ago, it wasn't given during church service, it was sent in a big envelope just like this one." He pointed to the flat envelope on the table.

"Oh. Why didn't you tell me about the first one?"

"I didn't want people all in your face; the less you knew the better. I didn't want you to have to pretend not to know when you did. That would have been too much pressure on you."

Loretta nodded.

"Now that we've had all this commotion with the church and the spotlight on the news, you're used to getting the questions. So, there won't be much that can catch you off guard, I hope. Just keep answering the way you've been doing." He grabbed the envelope. "I want you to open it."

"What, you think this envelope is from the same person?"

"How often do we get FedEx envelopes sent to the house?"

She thought about it. "Well, I don't remember us ever getting one, now that I think about it."

"Exactly. I may be jumping to conclusions but what else could it be?"

"I don't know Honey, but there may be a perfectly good explanation. Are you sure you still want me to open it?"

He nodded and finally sat as well.

Loretta opened the envelope and peeked inside. She grabbed the sheet of paper that was inside and placed it on her lap then reached back in and pulled out two envelopes. "It's a letter, addressed to you." She tried to hand it to him, but he shook his head.

"No, you read it."

She began reading it to him. A proud smile appeared on her face. As she kept reading a few tears rolled down her cheeks. When Loretta was done, she handed the letter to her husband, who wiped his eyes with the back of his hand.

"Do you want me to open these too?"

Pastor David shook his head.

Loretta reached inside her side table and retrieved a letter opener. She looked at her husband again before pulling out the envelope's contents. He nodded his reassurance. She slowly pulled the cashier's check out, saw that it was made out to His Way Church, and gasped, her eyes doubling in size. She quickly looked up. She reached to give it to him, and he stood to get it. Before he could look at the check, Loretta broke down in tears. Pastor David turned the check so he could read it. His knees buckled from the amount of zero's he saw, and his body hit the floor. He let out a yell, not because of any pain his knees felt, but because the shock was so great, he released it into the air.

Loretta sunk to the floor and crawled over to her husband. They cried and held each other for a long time, almost forgetting about the other envelope. Finally, Pastor David pulled Loretta up to the seat and they sat there not saying a word. Loretta noticed the letter opener had dropped to the floor which reminded her of the other envelope. She looked at her husband through pink eyes. His eyes gave her the OK to open it, but she shook her head. He sat there staring at the envelope, then swallowed hard. He walked over to the couch, picked up the fallen letter opener and placed it on the side table. He picked up the envelope and sat, glaring at his wife, both of them unaware of its contents. He turned the envelope over and opened the top with his finger. He pulled the check out and glared at it. His eyes blinked rapidly then he shot up. He didn't believe he had any tears left in him, but they came out in a bawl. He ran around the house waving his arms and hitting them against his legs still clenching the check that had been made out to him personally. After many laps, he breathed hard and went to sit by Loretta. Her eyes, still colored with gratefulness, looked at him in question. He straightened out the check and handed it to her while saying, "We're going to be just fine."

***

Frank and Laura sat at the kitchen table, Frank browsing news headlines on his tablet and Laura looking through her phone.

"What do you think Pastor will do with the money?"

Frank lowered his tablet and smiled. "I don't know, plenty of things. That's if he lives through the shock. All those zeroes on that check, might make his heart skip two or three beats."

They both laughed uncontrollably.

"I hope he gets off that job and takes early retirement," Laura sipped her tea.

"He just might. If that check doesn't convince him, nothing will."

"You think he'll buy a car?"

"I'm sure he'll pay his house off first. I don't know how much he owes on it, but he'll still have plenty left to buy two or three cars if he wants to."

"What do you think; Mercedes, BMW?"

"Nah, maybe for Sister Wright if that's what she likes but he's probably not gonna want to get something too expensive. He doesn't want to have something so out of line from most of his members."

"Or he can show them what God can do and how he blesses."

"True," Frank shook his head, "but whatever he chooses, he deserves it."

"Absolutely," Laura smiled. She waited a few moments then touched Frank's hand. "I'm proud of you for taking care of your mom."

Frank nodded and patted her hand in return. "Long overdue."

C28

THE GROUP OF pastors sat around the table of a small café. Pastor David put down his cup and looked around the table at his fellow laborers in the Gospel. "I need you all to pray for me. Tomorrow at church, I'm going to do something pretty unorthodox, for me anyway."

"What is it?"

"I can't tell you yet. I'll tell you next time we meet."

"Why?"

"Because I don't want any of you to talk me out of it or tell me to wait. And I don't want to start second-guessing myself. I mean I don't want to be disobedient, because I clearly heard from God."

"Then what's the problem?"

"It doesn't make sense," Pastor David leaned back.

"Then it probably is from Him," Pastor Henry took a sip of his drink.

A soft laugher was barely audible.

"Now, that's true. If it's not easy and if it *doesn't* make sense, you can pretty much bet, that's God's will."

"Oh, my goodness yes. I told someone just the other day, 'since He told me to do this, you'd think He'd make it a little easier,' but His ways are not our ways, His thoughts are not our thoughts."

"Amen to that."

"Speaking of prayer, I want to thank you for praying for me with that TV interview. I can't tell you how much of a miracle that was. I mean this lady was ruthless; first coming up to the church moments before bible study, then showing up on Sunday morning asking the members all kinds of questions, oh, and her camera man slipped into church apparently after the deacons asked her to leave and even in the interview, she tried to make me look some type of way, trying to paint me in an unfavorable light, and I thought for sure she was going to slice and dice that footage to make me look like a fraud or something, but she surprised me. She didn't fool around with the taping at all and she played the whole interview."

They all looked at each other then looked at Pastor David.

"What?" David asked They were clearly keeping something from him.

"We did pray but it was more than that," Pastor Keith responded.

"What do you mean?"

"You didn't tell him?" Pastor Henry questioned Pastor Anthony.

"Tell me what?"

Pastor Anthony removed his hands from the table and slowly rubbed the top of his legs, avoiding eye contact.

"If you won't tell him, I will." Pastor Henry said.

"Wait a minute; you all know something I don't."

Pastor Henry and Pastor Keith looked at each other and said "Yes" with the joy of mischievous twins.

Pastor David fell back in his chair not knowing what to think or what was about to be said.

"You know we all saw the other news reports, but we couldn't do anything about it. Well, turns out, Pastor Anthony here, could." Henry looked at Anthony urging him to take over the conversation.

Pastor David took a quick glance at Pastor Anthony then returned to Henry and Keith.

"Isn't the Lord good? I mean won't he come through?" Pastor Keith joked, deliberately taking a long time to answer, as Pastor David squirmed.

"Pastor Keith, if you don't hurry up." Pastor David playfully warned.

"Alright, alright. See, Pastor Anthony took action. I didn't know this beforehand; did you know about it?" Keith looked at Henry.

"No, I didn't know about it. And you didn't know about it," Henry directed to Pastor David who bit his lip as Pastor Henry joined in the shenanigans of Pastor Keith.

"Keith!" David shouted.

They both laughed as Pastor Anthony shook his head.

"OK, for real this time. I'm serious." Keith cleared his throat for emphasis. "Pastor Anthony called one of his members, who just happened to work as an editor at the news station. Being a tenured employee, she wasn't intimidated by Robyn in the least. She confronted Robyn on her plans and thwarted them, then oversaw the project herself and made sure it was done right, truthfully, and without malice. Then, she went to

Robyn's boss and convinced him to end the entire series."

"You did that for me?" Pastor David's mouth fell open. "You are good for something; I don't care what these guys say about you."

They all laughed this time.

Pastor Anthony finally broke his silence. "Henry told me what happened in the interview, much more than you said, I might add," he directed to Pastor David, "and I wasn't about to let anyone make a mockery out of pastors or The Church."

"Hey, I'll take it." Pastor David jumped up and nearly tackled Pastor Anthony in a hug.

Pastor Anthony's body froze. "Uh, OK Brother, let's not get beside ourselves."

David regrouped and sat back down. "You don't know what that means to me. I really appreciate that."

Anthony nodded.

"I thank all of you. And thank you, Lord." David exclaimed.

C29

THE CHOIR WAS especially anointed this Sunday morning as they sung a mixture of contemporary and traditional gospel songs. Pastor David came out later than normal but was able to hear the last song. To all in the church pool's surprise, Jorge and Maria came around the corner as well, right behind the pastor, and stood in the front row. Maybe Pastor had spent the last few minutes trying to persuade them to stay, to no avail. Or maybe time was spent because he was sending them off with a profound prayer and his blessing. No doubt they would give a testimony and formally say their goodbyes to the church they had called home for many years.

Mixed emotions reverberated throughout all the members of the lottery pool as they faced the inevitable, losing a couple who had become really close friends. Maria was a wise woman who wore the role of mother-figure to the ladies, with grace and humility. She was always eager to have them fellowship at her home and she always wanted to cook them a meal. They would miss her stubbornness as she always fought them from trying to wash the dishes afterward. She was the ultimate host.

Jorge was laid back and could always be counted on to throw in a word or two from his native dialect when you least expected it. He'd add some bonus words now and then just to get under Craig's skin, which gave extra entertainment to the fellas.

After the choir was finished Pastor David grabbed a microphone and stood near the top step. He announced that Jorge and Maria were doing a great work in Mexico and invited them to share their testimony. Both Jorge and Maria spoke about the work being done and the difference in the lives of those in their Mexican community back home. The pictures that scrolled on the screen behind the choir stand gave clarity and a realness that words could not. After they spoke, the congregation had a deeper appreciation for their ministry. Jorge gave the microphone back to Pastor David as Maria went to her seat.

"Hold on Ms. Maria. If you can come back over here, I want to tell you both something. I want to publicly tell you both how proud I am that you are doing the work of the church." Then he addressed the congregation. "This is an example of ministry, going beyond these four walls and meeting the needs of people where they are. This lovely couple met with me in private earlier and we've also interacted while they've been gone these past months, so I have a close understanding of what they've been going through. It's not easy but it is worth it. Now I want to tell you two in front of everybody, what the Lord told me."

They looked at each other then back at Pastor David, who looked them both in the eye. "I feel led to offer the church to Brother and Sister Garcia to start a Spanish-speaking service."

Jorge and Maria's faces froze.

Reading their expression, Pastor offered up, "I don't understand it either. Yeah, you all heard what they just said about starting their ministry and all the plans they have for it. I'm not dumb."

The congregation laughed.

"And I'm also not crazy enough not to obey God's voice. He told me to offer it to you. We can work out the details later. You can use the church any time after our services are over. Or if you choose, you may not want a service on Sunday. It's up to you. Now, however you respond to this proposition is your business. I've done my part."

The congregation erupted with applause and encouraging sentiments as Maria used her index fingers to wipe her tears and Jorge's head fell from the weight of the invitation.

***

Laura answered her mother's call on the first ring. These days, when she saw her mom's name come up on her phone, she hesitated, having a quick concern of whether her dad was alright or not. That was a scare she did not want to relive. "Mamma, is everything alright?"

"Yes, baby, your dad and I want you three to come to the house tomorrow night for a family meeting. We have some things we need to discuss with you all."

"OK, but what is it about?"

"You'll find out when you get here…it will be OK Laura."

Right, then just tell me. You and Daddy have sent me through enough surprises already. Laura closed her eyes. "Did Maury do something?"

"No."

"Is it because of Maury?"

"Laura."

Her mom's tone as she called her name said the unspoken, *don't ask me anymore questions, just do what I asked.* So, there was only one response Laura could give, "OK, I'll be there."

Laura didn't even bother talking to Frank about her concerns regarding this. Family meetings were meant just for her parents and their children, so Frank wasn't invited anyway. This gave off so many alarm bells in Laura's mind, but she kept her reservations to herself. Frank was well versed with her feelings regarding her brother and his many vices. She was tired of talking about her family issues anyway. It was draining her. She had focused too much energy in not only trying to keep quiet about giving her parents the money, but also trying to help them keep it for themselves by protecting them from their own son. And now her dad's health added to the mix. He wasn't the best at saying "no" to Maury but at least he was some type of barrier Maury had to consider before coming up with his schemes. If something were to ever happen to their father, their mother would be totally unguarded from whatever Maury's mind could conceive.

She thought for a moment about what their parents could possibly need to discuss now. Their mother had already dropped the bomb on Laura that the house was now going to Maury, what else was there? Her mouth opened. The thought had just occurred to her. Would her parents be so naïve to leave the money that Frank and Laura had anonymously given them, to Maury too? If that were the case, she would absolutely come unglued. There was no way she would stand for that. And if they didn't take heed to her objection, since she was the executor of the will, she would make sure that she got her money back, one way or the other. And she wouldn't feel the slightest guilt about doing so. If her parents knew she was the one that gave them the money, they wouldn't hesitate to give it back to her, the rightful owner in the first place. But since she could never tell, she'd have to fulfill what she knew in her heart their wishes were, her way.

***

Frank sat in the chair beside his mother's bed, watching her sleep. The text alert made his phone vibrate. As he opened the text, the picture of the car he had been wanting to get, engulfed the phone screen. He simply responded by typing, *something's come up. I've got to put this on hold.* Knowing his mother's condition had changed him. Knowing what he had done and didn't do got the best of him. At first his regret had overtaken him so, that he spent many nights with his mother. He had to try and undo some of the damage he had caused, some of the neglect that he had ensured was there. All the ill will he had felt toward his mother turned into hatred for his father, but he eventually realized none of it even mattered. All the negative emotions wouldn't change anything, and it wouldn't redeem any of the time he had lost. It wouldn't bring back his father and it wouldn't heal his mother. He learned that he'd have to be thankful for the now. He prayed for her to get better and the doctors' assessments were encouraging but they could only do what they knew how to do. Only time would tell. However much time she had left, whether it would be a couple years or many more, he was going to make sure his mother wanted for nothing. And he was grateful for the chance to make things right.

***

Laura sat in the driveway of her parents' home. Maury and Nell were already there, as evidenced by their vehicles, Nell's a five-year-old Honda Accord and Maury's a six-year-old Nissan Maxima, the passenger door a different color than the rest of the car. Laura strategically parked behind Maury. If he were to try and leave out of there quickly, he'd have to wait for her. She didn't know what to expect out of this, so at least she could control any escape attempt he had planned and maybe talk some sense into him. "Lord, please give me strength to deal with this," Laura grabbed her purse and headed for the front door.

She rang the doorbell before unlocking the door with her key. She heard chatter coming from the den and announced her arrival. When she walked into the room, she said hello while taking inventory of everyone's expressions, paying close attention to her father's. She noticed that in the past, anytime Maury pulled a fast one on them, her father would look away from her. She wasn't sure if it was the shame of him not being able to stop his own son, or the shame of not being able to stop his own wife from giving in to their son. Today, she couldn't detect anything from her dad's expression, one way or the other, but Laura wasn't sure if that was because of his impaired health or not. She did notice papers sitting next to Maury and her look to him said, *what in the world have you done now?* His blank stare was the unspoken response. After hugging her parents, Laura took her seat and waited.

"It's good to see all my children together," Tom smiled.

Maggy shook her head as she rubbed Tom's leg.

"You really gave us a scare, Daddy." Nell crossed her arms.

"You?" Maggy looked from Nell to Tom. "I was terrified."

"Alright, alright, I've got it under control now. I'm doing everything the doctor says. I'm eating better and exercising; you're not getting rid of me just yet. But it's a good reminder of how fast things can change. And believe it or not, I think it was a blessing in disguise. We've all had a wake-up call, right son?"

Maury nodded and looked around the room. "Well, I guess that's my cue." He grabbed the papers Laura had eyed and cleared his throat.

Oh, here we go. Jesus, don't let me hurt him. Laura quietly started cracking her knuckles one by one. She stole a glance at Nell but could tell from her expression she didn't have any idea of why they were there either.

"Relax Laura." Maury could see the tension on her face, but his words gave her no comfort. "Alright, now I'll admit I've done some things in the past. I'll give you that, but you know, daddy's situation, it really did something to me. And the way you looked at me at the hospital," he directed to Laura, "you thought it was my fault he was in there. At first, I was pissed. Oh, sorry Mamma. I was mad, but when I really thought about it, and it took me a few days, I really couldn't say for sure that I didn't have something to do with it. And I don't want to be the reason that something happens to either one of you. Mamma, I saw the worry on your face, and I don't want to see that anymore, and think that I possibly had anything to do with it. What I'm basically saying is, I know I need to step up, so I need to step down first."

Nell tilted her head.

"Dad and I have been talking a lot since all this happened," he motioned his hand toward Tom, "and I've talked to Mamma too. And you'll be glad to know that I've asked them *not* to give me the house. I want The Will to stay the way it is. I don't want y'all to hold a grudge with me, thinking I'm trying to get over on you."

"I appreciate that, considering I had no idea that was ever discussed. So, what are the papers for?" Nell glanced at them. Laura was glad she asked, to keep her from doing so. Maury still wasn't through talking so Laura's feelings teetered between caution and optimism.

"It's a copy of The Will. I made sure Mamma and Daddy changed the house back to splitting it evenly between us and I asked Mamma to get me a copy of it so I could show you two." He paused, expecting his sisters to interject but they were silent. "That's it. No surprises. I hope you can already see a difference in me, just from what I've been doing around here. I know it may take some time for y'all to really trust me, but I can tell you I'm a changed man."

Maggy's smile was one of hope and Tom slowly reached out his hand to shake Maury's.

Nell stood to show her support with a hug while Laura watched, inwardly wanting to get a hold of the will so she could read it for herself. But that would have been rude and would spoil the moment, all while making her look bad. She would have to be patient; she was still the executor, so she'd get the copy soon enough. But now she needed to support her parents' renewed hope in Maury, even though she felt it would be short lived. Maury looked at Laura, who was still seated, not knowing what her next move should be, her thoughts such in overdrive that it paralyzed her. All sound was sucked out of the room as Laura, for the first time since she had arrived, really looked into her brother's eyes. They lay bare, vulnerable, without pretense, inviting her to examine him, his words, his look, his demeanor, anything…and everything. He opened his hands as if to show her he had no weapon, no armor, and no motive, nothing to hide. Maury stepped over to her and lifted her arm pulling her into his embrace. He whispered into her ear, "I'm serious and I'm sorry." He held her until her doubt and negative feelings toward him eroded away like pressure slowly being released from a pipe. He refused to let go. She had no choice but to let her shoulders sink into his embrace. Having her brother's arms around her released tension she didn't know she had. She was amazed at how quickly and through such unusual circumstances God had answered her prayer.

C30

JEROME PARKED THE car and went around to the passenger side. He took Tammy by the hand, lifting her out of the seat, and walked her around to the front of the house. He loosened the knot on the handkerchief that wrapped around her head and placed it in his pocket. "Open your eyes." Tammy's mouth opened simultaneously with the widening of her eyes. She glanced at her husband then back to the house, slowly shaking her head. Jerome smiled and took her by the hand.

"My lady, your dream house awaits."

Nestled on their own track of land, two acres right outside Porter, a small town on the north side of the city, Tammy finally saw the finished product of she and Jerome's vision come to life. Her eyes surveyed the massive structure in front of her, from the red roof to the large windows to the three large individual doors that shaped the garage. She turned a complete 360 degrees to view the sea of plush green that the cobblestone driveway divided. "You did all of this?"

"Me and my team took care of the house, but I hired a landscaper for all of this." He motioned to the meticulously manicured shrubs and colorful flowers that were speckled throughout the lawn. "Come on, there's more to see inside."

Tammy focused on the intricate glass inside the wooden door as Jerome pressed his thumb down on the latch, gaining entrance into their new home.

"Oh, it's so big," She gasped at the open space.

"It's the high ceiling."

"How many bedrooms?"

"Four, with four and a half baths; I remember."

"You did much more than that. I love it, thank you!" She lunged into him, gripping him.

"You're welcome," he laughed.

He grabbed her hand and pulled her forward. "I have a surprise for you." He quickly ushered her toward the back door.

"Wait. This is my kitchen?" The rhetorical question echoed from the ceiling-high cabinets and circled around the island then rested on the long counter that overlooked the living room. The petite counter in her old apartment didn't even compare to this one, sitting five over-sized high-back chairs comfortably. "OK," She looked at Jerome and proceeded.

He opened the back door and they walked outside. "Your oasis, my love."

"Oh wow, this is amazing. This…I don't have words for this." Her head darted from the brick back porch furnished with chairs that doubled as an entertainment hub and barbeque headquarters, with the flat screen television nestled in the wall, and built-in pit along the outer edge overlooking the lawn. "Jerome, this is far beyond what I hoped for."

"I'm glad you like it. Let's go look at the rest of the house."

"I'm so glad I changed hospitals, now I'll only be fifteen minutes away from home. And my part time schedule was approved as well."

They both vowed to work fewer hours so they could enjoy each other and planned extensive travel around the world, their first booking in Greece, followed by an Alaskan get-away.

"Good, let's get this traveling out of the way so I can finally meet my kids."

Tammy shook her head. "Don't rush it. You said you'd give me five years to travel as much as we want to, and then concentrate on starting a family."

"Yes, by all means we can travel as much as you want to. That's your thing. But I'm counting down the days 'till we get started on our family. We need to fill these rooms up."

Jerome grabbed her and pulled her close. "We could christen one of the rooms right now." He gave Tammy a passionate kiss as her shoulders sunk into his embrace.

***

Jorge knocked on Pastor David's office door at the church and he and Maria listened for the invitation to enter.

"Awe yes, I've been waiting on you two. Please have a seat."

"Thank you so much, Pastor."

"I'm so glad you took me up on my offer to start the Spanish-speaking ministry."

"It was only after much prayer."

"Yes, of course, you can't rush into anything like this."

Jorge nodded. "And the second service time slot is perfect."

"Alright. And what did you decide to do with your church in Mexico?"

"Now we'll have a church in two locations." Jorge's face turned a shade of red.

"That's wonderful, brother. Listen, that's nothing to be ashamed of or shy away from. The number of churches or the number of members doesn't faze me because God is in control of all that. Don't ever feel like I'm threatened by your success because I'm secure in who I am. I'm just happy for you; for the kingdom. So how are you going to maintain both?"

Jorge gave a knowing shake of the head, very aware of the immense responsibility of having locations in two different countries. "My brother Manuel took on the responsibilities as overseer of the church in Mexico, but I kept ownership. He's doing a great job. I'll continue to monitor his leadership because I'm open to the possibility of releasing the ministry and ownership of the building over to him."

"Very well. Continue to pray about that. And I'll be praying for both you and your brother. You can share the great news with our church this Sunday and when you're ready, let us know the date for your first service. I'll support you and Maria in any way that I can."

***

Maria couldn't wait to tell The Pool about the decision to start their ministry at the church and everyone wanted to celebrate Jorge and Maria's next chapter, so they gathered at their home. Seated in the couches around the room, gave everyone the opportunity to catch up with each other.

After they all circled around Jorge and Maria and prayed for their success Craig started in on Jorge. "And Jorge, you'll never have to worry about me coming to visit your services."

"No problemo."

Laughter broke out. "Man, that's about the only Spanish word I've ever understood you saying." Craig could always be counted on to lighten the mood.

"If you come, I bet you'll learn how to speak the language."

"I don't want to know, Jorge. Y'all can have it."

Don shook his head.

"Speaking of ministry," Jerome piped in, "Tammy and I agreed to help mentor a few young married couples."

"We're just going to do a test run right now, just two or three. We're pretty green ourselves so we don't want to get in over our heads," Tammy interrupted.

"Wow that's great. What's the story on that?" Laura's excitement was evident.

"We're just helping out Don and Janet," Jerome added.

"What do you mean?" Laura asked.

Don sat up and grabbed Janet's hand. "We hadn't told anyone yet but we're starting a marriage counseling ministry at the church."

"What?" Laura's outburst and open mouth reflected the unspoken surprise around the room. "Where did that come from? I mean it's great, but what?"

Janet chuckled. "I know, kind of a shocker for us too but after everything Don and I went through in our marriage, we just want to help other marriages be stronger."

"And I'm sure none of you know this, but they've been helping us with our marriage," Tammy smiled at Jerome, so we want to give back and hopefully make a difference."

"One thing we've learned in our short marriage, is it takes more than love to make it work," Jerome tilted his head downward for emphasis.

"That's wonderful news," Maria clapped her hands.

"Any classes on dealing with exes?" Amanda sat up.

Craig grunted.

"Uh oh, what happened?" Maria put down her glass.

"You guys know Josh decided to live with us while he goes to college," heads nodded, "well come to find out, Gloria, that's his mom, asked him to co-sign for a car."

"Wait a minute, she asked her son, who's barely an adult, to co-sign a loan?" Don shook his head in disgust.

"Yes, she most certainly did," Amanda's eyes grew wider than her voice grew louder.

"What did you guys do?" Tammy asked.

Craig let out a sigh from his belly. "I had to sit down with him, and we had a long talk, about everything. I just had to tell him that sometimes you have to love people from a distance. Even though he loves his mother I had to let him know that what she was trying to do would ruin him and that he would have to set some boundaries with her."

"Wow. Did you say anything to her?" Janet asked.

"No, it wouldn't have done any good. If anything, she would have got on *his* case for telling me. And I don't want him to feel caught between the two of us. I want to make sure he stays comfortable talking to me about anything. I told him how he should handle it, and what to say, but he had to have the actual conversation with her on his own."

"Man, that's messed up," Frank resituated himself.

Craig wondered for a second if he should let them know Gloria asked him point blank if he'd won the lottery, but he didn't want to alarm anyone, so he decided against it. He had handled the situation already, so he felt it best to leave well enough alone. Instead he changed the subject. "What do you guys think Pastor Wright will do with the next check to the church?"

"Oooh, I don't know. It's a big one," Laura smiled.

"Wouldn't it be ironic if he gave some to Jorge's church?" Don said.

"Hmm, I never thought about that. That wouldn't be right," Jorge rubbed his chin, his eyes glued to the rug as if he were searching it for answers.

"Actually, that wouldn't surprise me. You know how generous he is," Frank said.

Sentiments of the same trickled throughout the room.

"Well, I certainly hope he doesn't say something over the pulpit again. We don't need any more publicity," Laura gave a look of warning.

"Ain't that the truth. That was a mess," Amanda folded her arms.

"Definitely a close call," Jerome took the opportunity to contribute.

"Too close," Tammy echoed.

"No, I think he's learned his lesson on that one. You just can't tell everything. Some things you just have to keep under wraps," Craig said.

"He may not even do anything right away. He may let things settle down and do something in a couple of years," Don offered.

"Like what?" Janet turned her head toward her husband.

"Something with the youth maybe or missions," he looked to Jorge for help.

"I…don't know," Jorge held up his hands.

"Jerome, you think he would build something else?" Frank asked.

"He certainly has a lot of options. With all the land around the church, he could do just about anything; bigger church, different building altogether for a separate non-profit, charter school, anything."

"I guess we'll just have to wait and see. And we may never know. He may decide to give it all to churches in third world countries, for all we know," Janet pondered.

"Well, whatever he does, it will be great," Laura said. That was something they all agreed on.

***

Pastor Wright tore open the envelope and quickly opened the letter. "Loretta! It came in." He left the envelope on the counter in search of his wife.

Loretta left their bedroom with half the load of clothes folded. They met in the hallway. "Loretta it's official," he handed the paper to her, "we've finally paid off the house."

"Thank you, Jesus!" Loretta grabbed his neck and held on.

"That's the first order of business. Now, you need to start looking for a newer vehicle. I told you I was going to upgrade your car."

"Since my last day at work is next month, I'm not going to be driving as much. You should be the one getting something new."

"No, I'm fine. I want you to have the better car. Now, I didn't say brand new, but it'll be newer than what you have now."

Loretta smiled. "What am I going to do with you, David?"

"Well, at least I agreed to go on vacation."

"You had no choice. That was my condition since you made me retire early. But it was a much-needed vacation you have to admit that."

He shook his head. "I don't know what I was missing all these years."

"I told you the church would go on without you."

"I knew it would, I just like being there. But you've been so patient with me. We've got a lot of catching up to do. What do you feel about taking one every year?"

Loretta's eyes swam with mischief. "Oh, we are. I've already booked a two-week European excursion."

"Two weeks!"

She cut her eyes at him.

He let his head fall as a sign of surrender. "You're not gonna hide my phone this time, are you?"

"It forced you to stay away from all the church responsibilities for a change, so you couldn't do anything but truly relax, that is, after your two days of worrying and complaining," her voice trailed off. "I know you may not see it but you're under constant pressure."

"I know you're right. And I appreciate what you were trying to do. I really did enjoy myself. And I do realize that I needed that."

David kissed Loretta on the cheek and held her close.

***

Pastor David returned to the pulpit after Jorge and Maria shared the news that they had indeed accepted the invitation to start a Spanish-speaking service there at His Way Church. "I have more great news to share with you. God continues to bless our church. I thank every one of you who are consistent in your giving by paying your tithes and offerings and for those who've just started tithing, please continue. Because of your commitment and generous giving our church has donated a great deal to other ministries in foreign countries, helped build more wells, sponsored mission trips, including one in partnership with Jorge and Maria's church in Mexico. We even established a scholarship fund for you the members who are attending college or trade schools."

More applause broke out. Laura smiled and stole a glance at Amanda and Craig. She couldn't wait to tell Frank, who had decided to spend the day with his mom.

"Right now, the deacons are looking into buying a couple of church vans to help with ministry and outreach. Now this last thing I'm about to tell you…" He swung his arms back and forth then looked at the musicians. "I'm gonna need a drum roll for this one."

Sister Loretta stood, smiling from ear to ear.

"Brothers and sisters get ready to shout. Tell your neighbor to scoot over a bit and give you some room."

Chatter increased as the congregation complied.

Pastor David signaled for the drummer to play louder. "My brothers and my sisters, His Way Church is now totally debt free!"

The church erupted as if the Houston Texans had just won the Super Bowl. Many screamed and yelled, jumping up and down or dancing. Shock adorned some faces. A few people had to ask their neighbor if they had really heard the pastor correctly.

"Yes, you heard me. We owe no man, nothing. Everything is completely paid off. Go ahead and praise him." The jubilation heightened as he continued, "Bless the lord with me, let us rejoice his name together. For he has done great and mighty things. He has done exceedingly above all we could ask or think. Blessed be the name of the Lord. Yes, Lord. Glory to your name." He took in all the excitement around the sanctuary. His smile couldn't get any wider.

"And to celebrate," he had to talk even louder in the microphone over the great commotion, "and to celebrate we are sponsoring a church cruise. The church will pay half the bill, for any member who wants to go."

The noise of shouts and screams erupted like it had been held back by a dam. It happened so quickly and with such magnitude, Pastor David had to take a couple steps back from the pulpit. It was a sight to behold. Mouths flung open, eyes widened, some grabbed each other and jumped up and down like school children who had just been told they were going on an out-of-state school trip. Don and Janet exchanged happy glances with the others in the lottery pool.

***

Laura sat on the couch in her living room and pondered the events that unfolded over the last few years that intertwined her and Frank's life with that of the four other families in the church lottery pool. They each had different hopes and expectations of what a win could bring them. Their journey confirmed some ideals and denied others. They each had their own surprising personal struggles that were enhanced by the huge windfall. But they each had crossed to the other side of their tests triumphantly and grown as a person and grew closer as a small tight-knit community that shared a common bond. Although some of their negative experiences were brought on by the fact that they had won, the truth was apparent that certain levels of maturity couldn't have been obtained under any other circumstances. Laura personally was grateful for the entire experience, even though she learned some things about herself that she wasn't so proud of, she dealt with her issues and grew stronger for it. She closed her eyes and let out a sigh of satisfaction, of new beginnings, and of new possibilities.

She opened the compartment in her purse and retrieved the small torn-off piece of paper, read the handwritten numbers one last time, and ripped it to shreds. She threw the pieces in the garbage can and rubbed her hands back and forth. No more guilt or second guessing. She had moved on. Laura took a deep breath, closed her eyes and heard a faint familiar sound; one she hadn't noticed in several months. She couldn't help but smile as she walked toward the window. Instead of opening the blinds she pulled the string that cascaded them all the way up. Then she carefully opened the window and became a captive audience of one, to her feathered soloist. Laura now listened not just with her ears, but with her heart. Her tears flowed as she allowed the Lord to speak to her and shower her with peace. She looked up toward the clear blue sky and without words, she responded with, *Lord, I thank you for…The Win.*

The End

Book Club Questions

1. Do you agree with Frank's decision not to divulge that Laura actually picked the winning lottery numbers? Does your decision change if you are one of the members?
2. Do you think Laura should do more for her extended family? What would that look like?
3. What plan or restrictions would you put in place if your lottery pool won?
4. Can you identify with Pastor Anthony's stand on gambling? Which pastor's perspective do you most agree with?
5. What is your position on a church-sponsored trip to a casino? What would such a trip say about The Church and Christians?
6. Do you support Pastor David's decision not to tell his wife about the first donation and love offering?
7. If you could choose which church pool member to be, who would you choose and why?
8. Do you think Pastor David handled the situation with Sister Evella correctly? What would you have done?
9. Do you think reporter Robyn Rogue was just doing her job as she sought out the answer of if there was a church lottery winner?
10. What do you think Pastor David should do with his generous love offering?

About the Author

SHALONDA MCFARLAND is an author, speaker, and Gospel recording artist. She has dedicated her life to the glory of God specializing in youth ministries where she has been teaching, speaking, and volunteering for over twenty years. Worst Witness Ministry, which Shalonda birthed out of her book and workbook A Christian's Worst Witness…From Being Broke To Being Blessed is focused on teaching Christians how to handle money God's way. Her articles on Christian finance have been featured in various church mediums and Christian publications, including magazines and journals.

Mrs. McFarland is a dynamic, heart-felt, action-provoking speaker, who delivers a biblically-based message diverse with everyday examples and strives to live out her personal brand of *serving by adding value and exceeding expectations.*

Shalonda and her husband Doug have five children, Rakaya, Doug Jr., Mariah, Jordan, and Melanie, and reside in the Houston, Texas area.

Note from the Author

I hope you have enjoyed the sequel, *The Win 2*. I certainly enjoyed writing it. Christians playing the lottery and the bigger question of whether churches should condone and even support all sorts of gambling is a very controversial topic. I tried to shed light on the many perspectives of it. I also wanted to bring up possible scenarios of the effect a lottery win can have on an individual, lottery pool, and the family and church they are connected to. I definitely wanted to make you think about if the dream that most people have of winning the lottery is really worth it. Thank you for going on this journey with me.

Please show your support by leaving a review for this book on Amazon and Goodreads by scanning the QR codes below.

If you would like me to come speak at your event or attend your book club meeting, I can be reached at:

Email: Info@ShalondaMcFarland.com
Facebook: Shalonda McFarland Ministry
Website: ShalondaMcFarland.com

Note from the Author

Made in the USA
Monee, IL
04 November 2026

67378959R00105